ABORTION
in
PERSPECTIVE

The Rose Palace
or
the
Fiery Dragon?

Donald De Marco

Foreword by Marshall McLuhan
Illustrated by William Kurelek

Hardbound
  1st Edition .... September, 1974
Paperback
  1st Edition .... September, 1974

ISBN 0-910728-06-7

HILTZ & HAYES PUBLISHING CO., INC.

6304 Hamilton Avenue
Cincinnati, Ohio 45224
Phone (513) 681-7559

To my parents and my wife, whose attitude toward their off-spring has always been in the right perspective.

FOREWORD

The Waste Land of T. S. Eliot is a compressed vision of the contemporary Life-in-Death and Death-in-Life. The Christian, through dying unto self, awakens to life — a Life-in-Death; whereas the people in the *Waste Land* are typically engaged in living a life that, although often fast-moving, is devoid of meaning — a Death-in-Life. Early in the "play" one of the "jet set" is "staying at the archduke's, my cousin's", and goes out on a sled in the high hills and states that rootless creed: "In the mountains, there you feel free./ I read, much of the night, and go south in the winter." Later, one of the lowly victims of metropolitan existence is socializing at a pub, and her friend comments, with worldly scorn: "Well, if Albert won't leave you alone, there it is, I said,/ What you get married for if you don't want children?" In a world of perpetual motion and high mobility there can be no meaningful community, since by definition, all we really have in common is the mobility; and the one thing we depend upon is change. The mobility itself is inseparable from our new affluent technologies which demand that we become their servo-mechanisms.

Wordsworth's quaint lament in the early nineteenth centry that "the world is too much with us", serves at least to remind us that the power and scope of the world has increased considerably since his time. When Sputnik put the entire planet inside a man-made environment of information, the world may have seemed to become much smaller, but it also became much more obsessive and demanding. The power of the world to invade every feature of our personal lives has been given a kind of medieval Morality Play treatment by the Watergate episode. It is almost as if we had revived "for real" the popular medieval narratives of the Falls of Princes. As the world manifests its credentials and rewards in ever more theatrical terms, it becomes ever more difficult for some to resist the world, while for others it becomes easier and easier to reject its sinister and shallow pretentions. Like our money, which is a "promise to pay", our advertising and P. R. only promise to pay promises.

Even theatrically speaking, the drama of the world has become more and more a mockery of merely human satisfactions, when it is quite evident that the richest people in the world have to become "hotel hermits" for security reasons, and when the most powerful people in the world lead lives of frantic uncertainty. Siegfried Giedion's classic work, *Mechanization Takes Command* (New York: Oxford U. P., 1948) reveals in an unexpected way the story of why so many people choose death-in-life (the merely human and seculiar way of the world). It is a lovingly and artistically studied account of how man has come to do more and more with less and less at the expense of robotizing his existence. There is a long and careful account of the mechanizing of agriculture, on the one hand, and of the making of bread, on the other hand. (He does not look at the wine process.) But the most telling pages are those in which Giedion minutely scrutinizes the Mechanization of Death in his study of the meat packers. The universal awareness of mankind has until now held to a ritual sense of death, even the death of animals. By the simple procedure of the ever-diminishing fragmentation of processes, however, it is possible to eliminate all pain and ritual and meaning in death. Belsen, and Buchenwald, and Auschwitz testify to the inevitability of gradualness and to the power of cleanly bureaucratic efficiency in the administration of death.

It is probably a mistake to isolate the abortion mills of current death programs from the seamless fabric of our worldly lives, which have become invaded by the death principle of minute attrition *via* fragmentation. The situation suggests that no mere disapproval of abortion practices could avail an iota against the technological movement of life towards a way-of-death. Let us consider for the moment one of our conquerors, the TV image itself. This image is constituted by innumerable pulsations of bits of light. What makes the image so enthralling and compelling is precisely the intervals or gaps between these pulsations. It is in these intervals, which people feel urged to fill, that their involvement with the action occurs. Just as action is in the *play* between a wheel and the axle, so too, our psychic and social lives find their action in the *play* between our identities and the surrounding world.

As long as there is the interval of "play" between man and his world, there is action and life; but when the interval between the spirit and the world closes, there is no more play but the fusion of stasis and death. Those who merge with the *mores* of the world lose this power to play and to laugh at the world and its pretensions.

When the human spirit feels drawn into the mesh of the man-made images of the electric world, it sacrifices its identity. Part of the process of transforming life into a way-of-death is to involve mankind in the universal surround of resonating intervals which turns the whole environment of existence into a kind of irresistable TV image. A consequence of this total involvement in the man-made environment is the loss of private identity. With this loss comes the sense of unreality and of irresponsibility towards our own and other lives. As people have become more deeply involved in each other technologically, they have acquired the "mass" or crowd mind, with its irresistible demand for sensation and thrill and death. Against this tide, the Church alone can prevail.

Marshall McLuhan

"Vice is a monster of so frightful mien, As, to be hated, needs but to be seen; Yet seen too oft, familiar with her face, We first endure, then pity, then embrace."

Alexander Pope, *Essay on Man II,* 217-220.

TABLE OF CONTENTS

PREFACE

Philosophy is unsinkable. You may submerge it in one place but it is sure to bob to the surface in another. Repress it in the conscious and it survives in the subconscious; remove it from school curricula and it reappears in radical manifestos; restrict it from programming and it shows up in commercials; retire it from journalism and it returns in comic strips.

Mell Lazarus's cartoon creation *Miss Peach* well illustrates this insuppressible quality of philosophy: From behind her desk Miss Peach asks, "You have a 'philosophy of life', Ira?" "Yes Miss Peach", responds a droopy-eyed, curly-haired tot in the second row, "It makes me think about all the problems facing humanity, and how troubled the world is." "Then it must be a dumb philosophy of life", snaps an alert-looking little girl from the fourth row, "My philosophy of life is 'Don't Think'."

"The most thought-provoking thing in our thought-provoking age", writes the philosopher Martin Heidegger, "is that we are still not thinking." The philosophy that avoids thinking is just as much a philosophy as the one which pursues it unremittingly. Everyone is a philosopher whether or not he wills, knows, or likes it. Philosophy is a universal human possession, be it positive or negative, confident or cynical, original or borrowed, creative or destructive.

What is not universal is the conscious possession of philosophy. The cinema's "Alfie", who matters, "What's it all about?"; and poetry's "Prufrock", who wonders, "Do I dare disturb the universe?", float through life unaware of the forces that moves them. Their tragedy is that they do not consciously possess themselves; their subconscious philosophies possess them. Philosophy is unsinkable, but for many it is a "wandering bark" that moves through life's unchartered seas with neither guiding star nor propelling oar. "The philosopher is Nature's pilot", states George Bernard Shaw, "to be in hell is to drift: to be in heaven is to steer." Philosophy is the art of producing steersmen.

My book is essentially and explicitly philosophical. It aims at bringing to light some of the deeper philosophical implications of the abortion issue which are seldom discussed and rarely recorded. Most works on abortion either avoid philosophy or treat it disparagingly. Philosophizing is quite often understood by the general public as synonymous with conjecturing, theorizing or even dreaming. All too often the court of the reading public judges biology, psychology, parents, religion or society as absolute reference points in resolving the abortion debate, while dismissing philosophy as irrelevant and immaterial.

Metaphysics, objective value, reality, truth and justice are considered factors which weaken and subjectivize an argumentation.

Nonetheless, every position on the abortion issue, explicitly or implicitly, directly or indirectly, consciously or subconsciously, involves a philosophy. To appreciate more fully the rhetoric of the abortion debate one must first learn to understand, within that debate, the language of philosophy. According to a Jewish proverb, a wise man hears one word and understands two. Philosophy is the second word. Though silent, it is the prevading spirit that gives character and value to any utterance. For this reason, philosophy has a function akin to poetry — which names the ineffable. Poets and philosophers, writes Heidegger, "dwell near to one another, on peaks farthest apart." The function of the poet is to name the holy; that of the philosopher, to think Being. Alfred North Whitehead remarks that at the apex of philosophy the languages of metaphysics and poetry become one.

Poetic citations are interspersed liberally throughout the following essays with the hope that poetry's underlying philosophy will deepen and clarify the philosophy which is presented in more explicit form. The rich philosophical mines of poetry are of inestimable assistance to the philosopher's prose. Samuel Taylor Coleridge, who masterfully combined poetry with philosophy, stated: "No man was ever a great poet, without at the same time being a profound philosopher."

The usual method of development employed in a study on abortion is linear, moving rationally and progressively from a beginning to a middle to a conclusion, each successive part inter-connecting with the next. In contrast, the format of my book is less linear than graphic, rather like a painted mosaic. Each essay, analogous to the pointillist's dot of pure color, has a vitality of its own which illuminates one area of the abortion spectrum. Collectively, the essays blend into a unified field, just as the painter's disjointed dots take on form and pattern.

Thus the reader may reject the conclusions of certain essays without at the same time rejecting a single underlying structure on which all the other essays are based; the reader need not understand the whole before he can appreciate any of the parts; the reader may read the book in any order he chooses.

Abortion is such a multi-faceted issue that it naturally resists being treated by a linear, sequential, and rational development. A single-line argumentation, no matter how carefully pieced together, cannot keep pace with the multitude of simultaneous interlacing and overlapping concerns about the nature of the foetus, the rights of the mother, the role of the father, the responsibility of the medical profession, the consequences of abortion, the relevance of religion, the significance of philosophy, the laws and attitudes of society. Moreover, a linear procedure is ill-suited to deal with the paradoxes that colliding social imperatives create: if parenthood is a right, is population control possible? if a woman has a right to abort, does a doctor have a right to be more than a technician? if a woman has a therapeutic abortion, is she free to refuse an accompanying therapeutic sterilization? if women overcome feeling guilty about their abortions, will they retain any respect for life?

A mosaic of essays is perhaps a more suitable form through which the community of ideas on the abortion issue can be expressed, because a mosaic itself is a form of community. The simultaneity of community and paradox eludes the rational thinker who develops his argumentation one step at a time. The entire vision of G.K. Chesterton is communal and paradoxical, because it is based on a consciousness of simultaneously disparate events and processes. Chesterton knew, writes Marshall McLuhan, that "analogy is community". Philosophy, poetry, metaphor and symbol are also "community". In an age when community, philosophy, and poetry have declined so far, the abortion controversy may very well reflect that decline.

In debating any issue intellectually (let alone one as complex as abortion) one tends to forget the nature of man. It is not the intellect which knows; it is man who knows by means of his intellect. Merely presenting knowledge or ideas, no matter how true, to the intellect does not guarantee acceptance, for it is man who must be convinced. Truth in its most serene and resplendent form does not appeal to the intellect unless it first appeals to the man. Impeccably logical arguments mounted on premises that are undeniably true are not necessarily persuasive, because man is more than a receiving set for knowledge. He needs to find things good as well as true. The intellect does tend towards truth, but its motion towards that goal will not be consummated unless man himself desires that truth as a certain good. Man's desire to know, his appetite that moves towards knowledge as good, is expressed through his will. Consequently, man refuses to know what he doesn't will to know, and consents to know only what he wills.

Nikolai Gogol's lament, "It is sad not to see any good in goodness", is an assessment of an infirmity of the will. Leslie Farber reaffirms this diagnosis when he concludes that the present era should be called the "age of the disordered will". The modern age suffers not only from intellectual deficiencies but from volitional ones as well.

Mindful that mere words do not convince the man, and that, as Oscar Wilde writes, "nothing of value can be taught", I present wrote the following essays with but a modicum of optimism. The eternal question, "Am I my brother's keeper?", must be answered by the heart. Scholarly investigations into the meaning and nature of 'brother', lengthy dissertations on the moral implicadions of 'keeper' — are all futile unless they prompt a loving response of the will. And no one can coerce another's will, cause it to respond as desired. The will is one's own. That is why all human improvement begins in the lonely self, not in the knowledgable treatise. Romano Guardini says it better:

> None of the great things in human life springs from the intellect; every one of them issues from the heart and its love.

Donald DeMarco
Kitchener, Ontario

I

THE FORCE OF PHILOSOPHY

"What philosophy essentially can and must be is this: a thinking that breaks the paths and opens the perspectives of the knowledge that sets the norms and hierarchies, of the knowledge in which and by which a people fulfills itself historically and culturally, the knowledge that kindles and necessitates all inquiries and thereby threatens all values."

—Martin Heidegger

—1—

THE RELEVANCE OF PHILOSOPHY

Philosophy can seem so curiously out of place in an age when specialization and expertise symbolize what is most progressive and relevant in a culture. The armchair philosopher and the ivory-tower thinker appear mythical and remote from reality when contrasted with today's hard-nosed realist: the white-coated laboratory technician, the fact finder, the trained specialist, or the research analyst. The philosopher seems a remnant from a pre-scientific age. He is a star gazer, a romantic, a dreamer, a visionary whose theories and opinions are largely conjectural, carrying little universal validity and virtually no authority.

The entrance of the philosopher into a contemporary controversy, then, such as that of abortion, draws scepticism and distrust. One of the commonest objections levelled against him is that he is short-sighted. He speaks of the unborn as if the unborn existed in a vacuum. He is apparently oblivious to both the distressing context in which the pregnant mother may find herself, and the presumed predicament the unwanted child may be in once he is born.

It is relatively simple for the philosopher to judge the immorality of the isolated act of abortion, compared to the agonizing decision of the mother who carries the unwanted child, or the struggle she must undertake in order to provide for him. The philosopher invests little of himself in his decision. He decides for another dispassionately, through his cerebral faculties. Whether he is right or wrong is an academic point to him. It is the other person, the object of his stern philosophical judgment, who stands to bear the painful consequences of his decision. Because the philosopher can opine without feeling, decide without vision, he can appear as contemptible and unsympathetic as he is irrelevant to such a complex and existential matter as abortion.

3

But this popular portrait is a caricature of the true philosopher who does not treat anything as if it were located in a vacuum. Neither does he treat others as if they were divorced from his own love for them. The philosopher, not being a specialist, sees a myriad of relationships which both join each being to another and are conjoined with the philosopher himself. Tennyson well expressed this sentiment when he wrote:

> Little flower — but if I could understand
> What you are, root and all, and all in all,
> I should know what God and man is.

The ancient Greek philosopher Pythagoras, who coined the word 'philosophy', also coined the word 'kosmos' which meant good, beautiful, orderly, coordinated, and whole, all taken together. The ancient Greeks knew of the interdependence of all things in the universe.

An ancient Chinese proverb reads, "Sexual intercourse is the human counterpart of the cosmic process." The Chinese also knew the universe to be a family. The very language of the Chinese attests to their fundamental grasp of reality as a web of relationships. According to D.T. Suzuki, a leading interpreter of Zen-Buddhism, Chinese adjectives always contain the implication of "for-me-ness". "The flower is beautiful" means "the flower is beautiful *for me*." The Chinese character for *good* (好) is the radical for *mother* (女) combined with the radical for *child* (子). (This is pronounced "Ho" in Cantonese, "How" in Mandarin as the third tone). The most manifest symbol of good, to their natural and intuitive thinking, is the pregnant woman. They understand good not as an isolated entity but as a harmonious relationship between mother and child.

For the deeply philosophical minded Chinese, the cosmos unfolds through material interaction; men and women love each other and beget children through intimate sexual union; the pregnant woman experiences a deep and abiding partnership with her unborn; the family is a closely knit entity; and society is a network of multitudinous relationships between families and various groupings. On every level of reality there is relationship; nothing stands in isolation. The Chinese symbol for good, the pregnant woman, is a prototype of good which pervades the universe and is echoed throughout human society. The unborn child belongs to the world because he is in relationship with his mother, who in turn is in relationship with her husband; they in turn are in relationship with their family, society, and the universe. No doubt this sense of everything's belonging to the universe is reflected in the Chinese tradition of assessing the child's age at one year at the time of his birth.

It is the Western scientist, not the philosopher or poet, who dichotomizes, cuts, separates, and isolates. Philosophers dis-

4

tinguish between things, but they do so only for the purpose of discovering an underlying unity. ,'Distinguish to unite" was the lifelong motto of the leading Thomist philosopher Jacques Maritian.

Most pro-abortionist arguments fail to consider the harmful social reverberations that legal abortion sets in motion. It is something of a mystery how a culture suddenly and over-whelmingly can be convinced of the importance of ecological balances on the subhuman level, and yet remain insensitive to the importance of ecological balances on the human level. Abortion shakes the universe. That is no exaggeration. For the want of a shoe a kingdom was lost. For the want of a proper regard for the human unborn, a civilization may be lost.

When the unborn is demeaned so that he can be dis-possessed of the legal justice which he is due, then sex, mar-riage, the family and society are also demeaned. If sexual union, at best, can produce only creatures which are of such low worth that they need not be treated with justice, then sexual union itself becomes sharply devaluated. Where sexual union depre-ciates, human love and the very meaning of life likewise depreciate.

Philosophy, as love of wisdom, seeks to discover the whole-ness of things through an understanding of inter-relationships. In matters of love, sex, and procreation, philosophy recognizes chastity as the wisdom of wholeness. The Russian word for chastity — *tselomudrie* — means by derivation "the wisdom of wholeness." Man is chaste only when he is complete. He is com-plete only when he discerns the nature and meaning of his pow-ers and uses them wisely in his relationships with others.

Society does not advance thanks to the specialist and the expert. The specialist is locked in his chosen niche, blind to the wholeness of things. The expert stays put, never progressing be-yond his microscopic field of study. Society will progress only when people learn to envision it as an integrated and organic whole rather than a haphazard sum of its specialized, mech-anized, isolated bits and pieces. The philosopher and the poet are understandably maligned and ostracized from a super-in-dustrial technological society. They are a positive menace to the assembly line, and a natural enemy to the forms of gov-ernmental administration which exploit the poor to fatten the rich.

Philosophers and poets indeed see so much, and con-sequently so much that is unjust, that there is reason to believe they are the ones who suffer most. Miguel de Unamuno, the em-inently learned poet-philosopher, saw life as an essentially tragic struggle between veracity and sincerity; between truth that is thought and truth that is felt. The grief he suffered for

5

his people at the outbreak of the Spanish Civil War exhausted him. In writing of Aquinas, Jacques Maritian exclaims, "Where is there a philosopher for whom anquish is not the companion of his destiny?" Pouring one's truest words into their truest molds only to find that what one said was treason to truth brings about profound anquish. But the suffering is in the philosopher, not inscribed in the philosophy. The philosophy must always be serene and objective. The philosopher's pain is between himself and God.

Aquinas has been callously labelled dispassionate, remote, and essentialistic. Yet his biographers record that he wept much. He pressed his brow against the altar, begging heaven for light and praying that his doubts might be dispelled. The contemporary philosopher of care *(Sorge)*, Martin Heidegger, has been flippantly referred to by his critics as "The Man in the Tower". Yet he, as well as Nietzsche before him, accepted philosophy as "a voluntary living amid ice and mountain heights." Nonetheless, Heidegger's concern for care between human beings is so great that he defines man's essential condition as that of care.

Heidegger adds that, "A philosopher is a man who never ceases to experience, see, hear, suspect, hope, and dream extraordinary things." These activities bespeak the philosopher's forward-looking dynamism. It is hard to imagine anything more abhorrent to his mind than the conservatism of the *status quo.* And what is legal abortion but a widescale acceptance of the *status quo?* Every pregnancy threatens to upset the *status quo.* To annihilate the child in order to return to an uninterrupted and predictable life stream is the most jaded form of ultra-conservatism. The advent of each child is a transcending of the past. It is the announcement that the past was not sufficient in itself. Returning to the state of the past imperfect is courageless, a fear of living life forwards, a death wish. Indeed, the society for whom the solace of the past has stronger appeal than its responsibility toward the unborn is itself possessed by a death wish. And who is to make such a diagnosis on society? It is not the philosopher? It was Friedrich Nietzsche who once wrote, "The philosopher is the physician for civilization." The most egregious oversight in the present age is governments' neglect to appoint a physician for civilization.

THE PHILOSOPHICAL ROOTS IN WESTERN CULTURE FOR THE PRO-ABORTION STAND

Every Westerner, from the moment he begins to learn, is exposed to the unseen danger of becoming 'Westernized'. To become 'Westernized' is to have achieved the infelicitous combination of a deep unawareness of the intellectual presuppositions of Western thought, and an authoritative posture that betrays a supreme confidence in their validity. When pervasive, this form of intellectual somnolence is critical because it prevents a people from properly understanding its culture and therefore from making needed corrections and improvements. A modernized Socratic admonition might read: "The unexamined culture is not worth perpetuating."

The abortion debate offers a case in point where it is common to find assertions treated as axiomatic while their presuppositions are regarded as non-existent. It would help bring a measure of respectability to the intellectual discourse on this most important and controversial subject, if the philosophical roots in Western thought which have shaped the major part of the pro-abortionists' intellectual thrust could be uncovered, understood, and evaluated within a realistic as well as Western framework.

Five major philosophical roots are set forth. They are: Atomism, Cartesianism, Existentialism, Empiricism, and Sociologism. To demonstrate that these roots have indeed shaped the pro-abortion mind, appropriate citations from the writings of significant pro-abortionists are presented. To help provide both illuminating criticism and a broader intellectual perspective, rejoinders are offered closing the treatment of each philosophical root.

ATOMISM: The history of Atomism begins in ancient Greece with Democritus, who believed that indivisible units called atoms (in Greek 'atom' means uncuttable) were the ultimate building blocks of the physical universe. He reasoned that if these atoms were unveiled, they would reveal the secret of matter and explain the laws governing its behavior.

The history of science from Democritus to the theories of atomic physics in the 20th Century chronicles the continuing drama of this search for the atom. Successive discoveries by such men as Dalton, Mendeleyev, Rutherford, Bohr, Fermi, and others provided increasing credibility for the existence of atoms. So convincing grew the idea that these indivisible units constituted reality that Atomism was transplanted from its natural soil in matter to a more ethereal home in society.

People were gradually liberated, thanks to the general spirit of Atomism, from thinking of themselves as belonging essentially to a class or a group, a church or a community; and took pride in the idea that they were, like atoms, entities unto themselves. Public and private life became more clearly distinguishable from each other, as did public and private morality. The Renaissance period and the Age of Enlightenment offered man a heightened sense of individuality and new reasons to take pride in his personal accomplishments. Rugged Individualism evolved; *Laissez-faire* capitalism flourished; the Age of the Common Man arrived. The individual had been born, and atomism was one of the handmaids who assisted at his delivery.

In order to secure individuality, rights were instituted. The founding fathers wrote the constitution of the United States inspired by such thinkers as Hobbes, Locke, and Rousseau, all of whose political thinking was strongly influenced by Atomism. Rights became absolute because individuality was the absolute essential character of man. Just as what was essentially real in the physical universe was believed to be the individualized atom, so too, what was essentially real in human society was believed to be the highly individualized man.

The less individualized members of society accorded unlimited adulation and envy to the self-made man, the star, the man of "conspicuous consumption", the man of property, the 'top dog', the tycoon.

ATOMISM AND ABORTION: The woman who conceives herself as primarily an individual insists that she be given the freedom to maintain that individuality. This freedom is logically extended to give her sovereignty over all aspects of her sexuality and reproductivity. Margaret Sanger declared in 1920, "No woman can call herself free who does not own and control her body." "No woman can call herself free until she can choose consciously whether she will or will not be a mother."[1]

Viewing the foetus as part of the woman's body, psychiatrist Thomas Szasz regards abortion as a crime "without victims":

> During the first two to three months gestation (when most abortions are performed), the embryo cannot live outside the womb. It may therefore be considered part of the woman's body. If so, there ought to be no specific laws regulating abortion. Such an operation should be available in the same way as, say, an operation for the beautification of a nose.[2]

In a similar vein, women's liberationist Alice S. Rossi writes:

> The passage of . . . a reform statute is only one step on the way to the goal of maximum individual freedom for men and women to control their own reproductive lives. Such freedom should include the personal right to undo a contraceptive failure by means of a therapeutic abortion. . .[3]

Phrased in the negative, freedom to maintain one's individuality becomes freedom from sexual servitude. Dorothy Kenyon, former municipal-court judge of New York exclaims, "For a state to force a woman to bear a child against her will is outrageous."[4] Lawrence Lader adds,

> To force these women to bear a child against their will, as a result of contraceptive failure, becomes the cruelest and most illogical sentence that society can inflict.[5]

Abortion, insofar as it protects a woman's individuality is seen as a private matter. Dr. Lawrence Kolb, professor of law, writes:

> Having an abortion is usually a very private matter. . . . A woman's right to privacy included her right to decide whether she would bear a child she had conceived.[6]

Dr. Alice Thompson, Dean of Women at Westford College, underscores the private nature of abortion:

> Even if she never considered the option [abortion] and never used it, she ought as a matter of principle know that she could. To deny her this right is a violation of her freedom as a person.[7]

The foetus, viewed as part of the woman's individuality, logically becomes her property to be disposed as she sees fit. Philosopher Ti-Grace Atkinson states that "Both her [the pregnant woman's] reproductive function and the fetus constitute her property."[8] Women's liberationist Barbara Sykes Wright, member of the National Organization for Women (NOW) adds:

9

Therefore I, and thousands upon thousands of women like me, believe that any law forbidding an abortion under good medical conditions is immoral and in addition unconstitutional, for it violates her right to control her property — her body — as well as her life, liberty and happiness.[9]

Applying the general philosophy of Atomism to the foetus, we easily see how the developing child could be interpreted as a threat to the individuality of the mother, especially when the mother does not conceive of her individuality in terms of involvement with a child. In addition, individual rights, because they safeguard that which is primary in man, are themselves primary. Therefore, an unwanted foetus, by interfering with a woman's individuality, would be violating her primary right to individuality.

REJOINDER: If the primary and essential character of man is his individuality, then the playwright is correct when he says, "Hell is other people." Human experience, however, shows loneliness to be the most unbearable pain man suffers; it shakes the very depths of his soul. The sense of what psychologists call "no-relatedness" is felt at the center of man's nature because man is destined to be more than an atomic unit.

The basic truth that man is inclined by nature to transcend the atomicity of individuality has been symbolized in many ways throughout hisotory: In the Hindu "tat tvam asi" (that art Thou); the pagan myth of the androgyn (the man-woman); and the Christian Triune God (Father-Son-Holy Spirit). The ancient Greeks lacked a word to distinguish private from public morality. The Romans taught that one man alone was no man at all. Modern philosophers of Personalism present man as essentially related to another in an "I-Thou" dynamic reciprocity.

If the need to overcome singleness through love, care and communication is rooted in man's nature, then the atomic picture of man is a false one.

CARTESIANISM: Rene Descartes, a 17th Century mathematician, came to philosophy with a sacred mission: to rescue philosophical thought from the shipwreck of scepticism and establish it once for all on the firm ground of indubitable certitude. He reasoned that philosophy would be preserved for all time if it could begin with a premise that was undeniably true and proceed unerringly according to a rigorous mathematical methodology.

The beginning was everything. Unless built upon a bedrock of certitude, the whole edifice of philosophy would ultimately crumble. Descartes set about his search for such a beginning by refusing to take anything for granted. He doubted everything.

The basis for his true philosophy would have to pass the most severe test. Applying his methodic doubt, he soon realized that although he could doubt everything else, he could not doubt the fact that he was doubting.

Thus he struck upon one of the most famous of all philosophical assertions: "I think therefore I am" *(Cogito ergo sum)*. Descartes' explication of his *"Cogito"* runs as follows: It cannot be doubted that I think. Furthermore, it is precisely this capacity to think that gives me the assurance that I exist. This is how I am essentially different from substances that can't think. I am a thinking thing and other substances which lack this capacity to think are mere extended things.

The double significance of Cartesian thinking to this discussion is the identification of what man is (his essence or nature) with consciousness, and the dualism by which body (extended thing) and mind (thinking thing) are classified as separate entities.

The influence of Descartes cannot be overestimated. Nearly all historians of philosophy agree that he fully deserves the title 'Father of Modern Philosophy'. Without some understanding of Descartes, modern thought is incomprehensible.

CARTESIANISM AND ABORTION: Philosopher Michael Tooley of Stanford University, writing in *Philosophy and Public Affairs,* employs a self-consciousness test to determine when a member of a species has a right to live.[10]

Professor P. F. Strawson points out that it is not unusual for people to regard consciousness as the identifying predicate of person.[11]

Moralist Joseph Fletcher so strongly supports a dualistic separation of moral personality from the body that Germain Grisez suggests his being "influenced by the mind-body dualism of seventeenth-century and eighteenth-century philosophy."[12] For Fletcher, neither personhood nor moral status are predicates of the consciousness-lacking human body.

> . . .a fetus is not a moral or personal being since it lacks freedom, self-determination, rationality, the ability to choose either means or ends, and knowledge of its circumstances.[13]

> . . .a patient who has completely lost the power to communicate has passed into a submoral state, ouside the forum of conscience and beyond moral being.[14]

According to Fletcher, "person" is non-existent in the absence of the synthesizing function of the cerebral cortex and before cerebration is in play.[15]

In a highly publicized incident in 1962, Mrs. Sherri Finkbine, who had ingested thalidomide during the second month of pregnancy, was denied a legal abortion in her home state of Arizona. Fearing that the foetus she was carrying would be deformed, she obtained a legal abortion in Sweden. In support of her mother's decision, Terrie Finkbine writes, "A man can think, dream, hope, and love. A fetus can't."[16]

Applying Cartesianism to the foetus, we conclude that since the foetus apparently lacks consciousness, it has no essential claim to being human. Also, the fact that body is not reducible to spirit nor matter reducible to consciousness precludes the foetus's being human. Therefore, to abort a foetus is not taking a human life.

REJOINDER: Rev. Charles Carroll, former Executive Director of the Center for Human Values in the Health Sciences at the University of California at San Francisco, writes:

> The wise man faces the fact that being precedes thought and, examining Descartes' popularly accepted dictum, *Cogito, ergo sum,* he wonders if the truth is not more likely reflected in *Sum, ergo cogito,* or better yet in *Sum, ergo cogito, ergo aestimo* — "I am, I think, I value." Surely, being precedes thought; and being and thought precede value.[17]

The Cartesian partition of thought and thing, soul and body, mind and matter, has taken its toll from modern man in various forms of intellectual schizophrenia, moral puritanism, and what Ralph Barton Perry has termed, "the ego-centric predicament".

The historical results of Cartesianism show conclusively that the separation of *thought* from *what is thought* causes man to lose his sense of feeling "at home" in the world. It has also led to the subjectivism of Kant, the idealism of Hegel, and the scepticism of Hume.

Had Descartes based his philosophy on "I love therefore we are," "I feel therefore I am," "I care therefore I am human," or even "I rebel therefore we are," he would have affirmed not only the self but the self in creative dialogue with "the other". Rather, Descartes incarcerated his philosophy in the sterility of the closed ego.

The logical philosophical antidotes to Cartesian egoism are: Heidegger's philosophy of "care" *(Sorge),* Blondel's "integral realism," Buber's primary word "I-Thou", Whitehead's "organismic philosophy," Marcel's "creative fidelity," Kierkegaard's "leap of faith," and Maritain's "knowledge through connaturality."

EXISTENTIALISM: The most popular and influential of all the innumerable forms of existentialism has been the one explicated by Jean-Paul Sartre. In addition to winning wide acclaim for his core of philosophical writings, Sartre has reached broad political, literary, and theater audiences through the dramatic means of his novels, plays, essays, and political statements. He has, in fact, amassed so strong an international reputation that in many circles his thinking has come to be identified with existentialism.

At the center of Sartre's existentialism is a radically novel concept of man. Foregoing use of the word 'man', Sartre chooses the expression "being-for-himself" *(Etre-pour-soi).* "Desiring to make himself" thus becomes the basic characteristic of the being who is conventionally called man. "Being-for-himself" is incomplete and seeks, through his conscious free choices, to overcome his incompleteness, define himself in time, and achieve an essence.

The relation between freedom and essence, therefore, is crucial. It is only through freedom and its authentic expression in free choice that the *"etre-pour-soi"* achieves an essence. One might ask what was the *"etre-pour-soi"* before it achieved an essence. Sartre's response is well known: "Existence precedes essence." One isn't human, or man, or animal, or substance, or anything at all until it can make itself or achieve its essence through free choices.

While the details of Sartre's philosophy are not widely known, his doctrine of the essential importance of freedom has been widely circulated and deeply felt.

EXISTENTIALISM AND ABORTION: Ashley Montagu formulates his notion of humanity as well as his defense of abortion by an expression as significant and succinct as Sartre's "Existence precedes essence." He writes: "Humanity is an achievement, not an endowment."[18]

Sartre's long time friend and philosophical associate Simone de Beauvoir reiterates the position that it is only through free choices that value and essence can be created. Accordingly, the foetus is yet to be valued; yet to achieve an essence.

> Creative acts originating in liberty establish the object as value and give it the quality of the essential; whereas the child in the maternal body is not thus justified; it is not only a gratuitous cellular growth, a brute fact of nature as contingent on circumstances as death and corresponding philosophically with it.[19]

In Sartrean existentialism the purity of the free choice determines an action's morality. Dr. David R. Mace, an abortion psychologist exemplifies this philosophy in counselling his cli-

13

ents. "It doesn't really matter what Helen decided," he writes. "Take your destiny into your own two hands," and make a choice you can live with comfortably in the coming years. He adds, underscoring the subjective aspect of the pregnant woman's agonizing decision, ". . .try to weigh the issues, and then list the three options in the order that seems best for you."[20]

Presbyterian theologian Herbert Richardson, emphasizing the importance of free choice in the determination of the nature of the foetus, writes:

> Indeed, within his value system [the person who has already accepted the value of technical control over sexual life] the primary mark of the humanity of the fetus is precisely that it is wanted and voluntarily created — not that it is unwanted, but somehow biologically complete. It is precisely his choosing it that creates his sense of responsibility for preserving its life.[21]

Sexual and career freedoms are also viewed as important enough to justify abortion. Dr. Henry Morgentaler of Montreal, who admits to having aborted more than 6,500 women between 1969 and 1973, argues that sexual freedom should exclude the burden of unwanted pregnancies:

> But if accidents happen — and they always will — women should be allowed to abort. After all, in the 1970s, females should have the same sexual freedom as males.[22]

Authors Lana Clarke Phelan and Patricia Therese Maginnis underscore the essential priority of career freedom over compulsory pregnancies:

> Abortion laws [that is, anti-abortion laws] are woman-control laws, or chattel laws, if you prefer . . .

> Forced by law into unending pregnancies and child care and rearing, most women had absolutely no opportunity to free their energies or money for other occupations.[23]

Application of Sartre's existentialistic conception of freedom and his doctrine of *"etre-pour-soi"* to the foetus, would make it appear that since the foetus has no freedom to overcome its incompleteness by making choices, it totally lacks any claim to essence or nature. Moreover, a foetus is not human where it was conceived by accident or through force since its value and essence could not originate apart from the creative liberty of the conceiving woman. Thus abortion, according to Sartrean thinking would not constitute taking the life of a human being.

REJOINDER: The principle "existence precedes essence" can be taken only metaphorically. It is one thing to say that nobody ever fulfills all of his potential. But it is quite another to say that a person has no essence at all until he fulfills a certain amount of that potential (Whatever that amount is remains unspecified. Sartre contends that if one did fulfill all of his needs he would become a "being-in-itself" [*"etre-en-soi"*] deprived of needs, freedom and consciousness).

If there can be existence without essence, what is it, then, that exists? Existence does not exist. Whatever exists must be something other than existence itself. This other something is the essence, nature, meaning or structure of that which does exist. Therefore, existence and essence are really contemporaneous; they have no reality apart from one another.

The fact that man is never fully developed, or fully free, or fully conscious does not mean that he is devoid of essence, nature, meaning, or structure. It is perfectly reasonable to suppose, as do many contemporary psychotherapists, that the meaning of man is to be always in the process of *becoming*. Nothing in this whole world is ever static, unchanging, or perfectly fulfilled. Furthermore, the nature of the existing foetus is intrinsically determined and is not conferred or withheld by the purity of his mother's free choice or by the degree of wantedness she attaches to her pregnancy.

EMPIRICISM: Empiricism is the broad area of philosophical thought dedicated to the perennially variated theme of 'seeing is believing'. The cardinal principle underlying Empiricism is that whatever sensation cannot verify is simply unverifiable. Empirical philosophers have always allied themselves with physical scientists, since both have an abiding enthusiasm for the observable and describable. Also they continually have prided themselves in opposing the armchair philosopher who creates a world of dreams and dogmas that are empirically unverifiable.

Because empiricist philosophers have emphasized observable and describable experience, they are known as 'realist' philosophers. The 'sensism' of David Hume, the 'utilitarianism' of John Stuart Mill, the 'pragmatism' of John Dewey, the 'positivism' of Ernst Mach, and the 'language picture theory' of Ludwig Wittgenstein are a few significant landmarks in the protean history of modern Empiricism. These schools have vehemently opposed less positivistic philosophies dealing with matters such as metaphysics, God, and moral values.

By applying the principles of Empiricism to the foetus, we note that the foetus is not a being with whom an adult can visually identify, especially in the early stages of foetal development. In the zygote, blastula, or gastrula stages, what can be observed, described, or experienced has virtually nothing in common with the human being known outside the womb. The assertion that the foetus has an unobservable soul which gives it a sacred value is purely conjectural by empiricist principles.

EMPIRICISM AND ABORTION: Strict empiricists reject as an unscientific speculation (if not as laughable) the claim that the microscopic fertilized ovum is a human being. They say that the embryo at any stage is "merely a blob of protoplasm," or "a parasite," or something going through a "fish stage" of development.[24] In addition, they label it a "product of conception" (Los Angeles Abortion Symposium, 1971), mere "tissue" (a John's Hopkin's Professor of Medicine), and a "growth" (a New York City abortion counselor). Fleming and Beebe state that until quickening, it is a live cluster of embryonic cells, and not a human being.[25]

What makes it particularly difficult for the empirical minded individual to accord humanity to the foetus is the lack of a common observable basis which would identify the two. The adult who is observed to enjoy a whole network of relationships and a wide variety of experiences does not resemble the relatively inert foetus in the least. As Rudolf Gerber notes:

> . . .no comparison exists between an adult acting in the world and an unborn fetus who has months to travel before achieving his first social act at birth.[26]

Sarvis and Rodman reflect a similar empiricist tendency when they write:

> It is much easier to empathize with an adult woman who strongly wants an abortion or with a woman who has been injured as a result of a criminal abortion than it is to identify with an unseen fetus.[27]

Thus, aborting a foetus is not taking a human life, because what is described by the ordinary empirical experience of man does not correspond to what is described by an empirical experience of the foetus.

REJOINDER: The essential limitation of Empiricism as an all-inclusive philosophy is that it fails to justify itself. The statement "Only what is sensed can be verified", itself is not sensed and therefore cannot be verified. We catch the radical empiricist trying hopelessly to jump over his own shadow. Einstein alluded to the limitations of Empiricism when he said that the most incomprehensible thing about the universe is that it is comprehensible. That by which a thing is known differs radically from that which is known. The measure and the thing measured are not one and the same. It is quite possible to comprehend certain universal laws and remain unable to comprehend that which allows comprehension; knowledge of the universe is not the same as the process by which the universe is known. Furthermore, Empiricism does not get to the *being* of things, nor is it concerned with their most fundamental attributes. Goodness, love, beauty, and truth — verities which nourish the very soul of man — transcend the limiting scope of the empiricist.

It is necessary, therefore, that some truths exist beyond the finite range of sense observation. Once we admit this necessity, we are able to approach with respect the thesis that what makes a man to be man involves the spiritual. It is not how he is *seen* but what he *is* that makes man a man.

The trouble adults have in identifying with the foetus is understandable. A similar empiricist bias has occurred historically throughout the entire field of medicine. Dr. Albert Liley writes:

> Because the medicine of adults preceded the medicine of the infant, neonate and foetus, a tendency has grown up in fields from surgery to psychiatry to start with adult life and work backwards . . . The net effect has been to consider the foetus and the neonate as a poorly functioning adult rather than as a splendidly functioning baby.[28]

SOCIOLOGISM: Sociologism is an extension of sociology. It seeks to establish, on a sociological basis, both man's meaning and his justification. It is acutely aware that without the redeeming grace offered by society, man's life degenerates to what Thomas Hobbes called a "state of nature" where men are driven above all else by "a perpetual and restless desire for power after power that ceaseth only in death." That which gives man a more elevated station, grants him a wider dimension, magnifies his importance, and refines his sensibilities is society. In short, society *humanizes* man. Without the blessing of society, man is either pre-human (pre-socialized), or sub-human (unsocialized).

In recognizing society's humanizing role toward the individual, sociologism does not ignore the welfare of the community. In fact, utilizing the axiom that the whole is greater than the part, sociologism stresses that the good of society transcends the good of any one individual. Therefore, with the humanization of man and the good of society in mind, sociologism interprets the meaning and justification of a human being as 1) participating in the process of humanization through the sum total of his inter-relationships with other members of society; and 2) contributing to the general good of society. An individual's life has no human meaning or human justification whenever he is pre-social; whenever he is of "no social stimulus value"; or wherever his own good contradicts the good of society.

17

In applying the general principles of sociologism to the foetus, we can appreciate that: 1) the foetus, being presocial, is not human; 2) the foetus, not being engaged in inter-social relationships, is not human; 3) the continuing life of the foetus, being detrimental to the mother, family or community, does not merit legal protection.

SOCIOLOGISM AND ABORTION: Dr. Edmund Overstreet, professor of obstetrics and gynecology at the University of California at San Francisco, speaks of legal abortion as being no longer merely a means of providing medical care, but as a form of sociological care for the community.[29] Niagara Falls abortionist Dr. K. Walker (pseudonym — W. Gifford-Jones) states that he does abortions for "sociological reasons." Glanville Williams writes that calling a zygote a human being would be acceptable "if there were no social consequences of doing so."[31]

Professor Garrett Hardin argues forcefully that restricting women from obtaining legal abortions would ultimately be "ruinous to the social system:[32]

> Is it good that a woman who does not want a child to bear one? An abundant literature in psychology and sociology proves that the unwanted child is a social danger.* Unwanted children are more likely than others to grow up in psychologically unhealthy homes; they are more likely than others to become delinquents, and . . . when they become parents they are more likely than others to be poor parents themselves and breed another generation of unwanted children.[33]

Hardin contrasts abortion with compulsory pregnancy and advises society to be more concerned about protecting itself from the presumed harmful effects of the latter than in chastizing women for their occasional sexual indiscretions:

> If [a woman] is pregnant against her will, does it matter to society whether or not she was careless or unskillful in her use of contraception? In any case, she is threatening society with an unwanted child, for which society will pay dearly.[34]

William Kopit and Harriet Pilpel, writing in a working paper for the New Civil Liberties Union Board of Directors, echo similar sociological sentiments:

---

* Hardin's claims here are conjectural and not to be taken as factual. There is no scientific evidence that would support his thesis that unwanted children are social dangers.

The enormous social costs* that the present 1965 abortion law create [sic] is clearly an evil that far outweighs any right to life that a fetus may be thought to possess.[35]

Philosopher Lorenne Smith emphasizes a cardinal sociologistic point when she justifies abortion by appealing to the supposed advantages abortion represents to society:

The advantages of abortion to parents and children in low-income groups, to women as a class, to society as a whole, clearly outweigh the disadvantages to the aborted foetuses.[36]

Therefore, under the principles of sociologism, taking the life of a foetus, if it were done in the interest of society, would not be illicit since the foetus does not possess the right to threaten or contravene the common good.

REJOINDER: If man's meaning and justification for living are conferred upon him by society, then there is no substantial basis in reality for such a conferral. Society, as such, does not have substantial being. Although it answers a natural human need, society exists by convention or agreement. Man precedes society in actual existence. Thus, the state exists for the benefit of man, who has substantial being, rather than man for the benefit of the state which has its being through convention or agreement.

The argument that it is justifiable to kill one in order to improve the lot of many is based on the fallacy that two lives are more important than one life. If each man's life is abolute, that is to say, *his* everything, then it is incomparable. Things can be compared to each other only when they have something in common. But the very thing one man does not have in common with another is his own center of existence upon which 'his everything' is either allowed to continue or is destroyed. Dostoevsky has argued convincingly that man should not bargain for even a lasting and perfect utopia if the price were the torture of one innocent child.

To describe man as pre-socialized or unsocialized is to speak of him from the outside of his being. Man's human nature, although it flourishes in a just society, is an inner essence and springs forward with the help of society not by the power of society.

To abort an unwanted child because he might later prove to be a disadvantage to society is to treat the innocent with more severity than the guilty; to give more weight to a fearful hypoth-

* Again, this remark is to be taken by the reader as purely conjectural.

esis than courage would allow, less hope for a positive reality than justice would require.

* * * * * * * * *

CONCLUSION: "Non omnes omnia possumus" (We cannot do everything for everyone) is a truism; however, it should not allow society to relax its efforts against the evil of one-sidedness. Individuality, consciousness, freedom, empirical science, and societal needs are indeed significant, but when isolated from their complementary values and raised to a level of unique significance, they merely illustrate a culture's immaturity. Whereas individual one-sidedness may be helpful to a society in offsetting and counterbalancing other forms of individual one-sidedness, collective one-sidedness is a different matter. Kierkegaard writes:

> But just as one generation affects round hats, and another prefers them three-cornered, so a fashion of the age promotes forgetfulness of the ethical requirement. I am well aware that every human being is more or less one-sided, and I do not regard it as a fault. But it is a fault when a fashion selects a certain form of one-sidedness and magnifies it into a total norm.[37]

It has been the genius of the West to divide and conquer. Each of the five preceding philosophies represents a one-sided and fragmentized approach to reality. *Atomism* separates the individual from the community and treats him as absolute. *Cartesianism* separates the ego from the other and man from nature, rendering their inter-relationships unaccountable *Existentialism* (Sartrean) separates existence from essence and makes freedom absolute. *Empiricism* separates the material from the spiritual and makes matter absolute. *Sociologism* separates the intrinsic from the extrinsic and treats the extrinsic as absolute.

If these varieties of Western thought are ever to be cured of their one-sidedness, they must first be examined at their point of origination. Many contemporary thinkers, having lost patience with the materialistic penchant of the West, have looked to the spiritual genius of the East to find the true philosophy of life. Others have sought a reconciliation of Eastern mysticism and Western materialism.

Wherever and however the solutions are to be found, the truth remains that no one is free who will not reflect. It is indeed ironic, as psychologist Carl Jung has pointed out, that "in the West there is as a great freedom politically as there is lack of it personally; whereas in the East we find just the opposite." Ac-

20

cording to an ancient myth, when Poverty and Plenty mated, Love was born. Perhaps when Apollo consents to dance with the Furies and the Furies permit themselves to bask in Apollo's sunlit reasoning, Truth and Peace will flower.

FOOTNOTES

1. Quoted by Lawrence Lader in *Abortion,* New York: Bobbs-Merrill, 1966, p. 167.
2. "The Ethics of Abortion," *Humanist* (September-October, 1966), p. 148.
3. Alice S. Rossi, "Public Views on Abortion," *The Case for Legalized Abortion Now,* (Berkeley: Diablo Press, 1967), pp. 31-32.
4. Quoted by Lader, *op. cit.,* p. 9.
5. Lader, *op. cit.,* p. 158.
6. David Mace, *Abortion: The Agonizing Decision,* Nashville: Abington Press, 1972), pp. 76-80.
7. Mace, *op. cit.,* p. 97.
8. Ti-Grace Atkinson, "Philosophical Argument in Support of the Human Right of a Woman to Determine Her Own Reproductive Process," 1967, quoted in Daniel Callahan, *Abortion: Law, Choice and Morality,* N.Y.: Collier-MacMillan, 1970, p. 462.
9. Testimony before the Governor's Commission in New York State for the Study of Abortion, February 29, 1968, quoted in Callahan, *op. cit.,* p. 462.
10. Michael Tooley, "Abortion and Infanticide," *Philosophy and Public Affairs* (Vol. 2, No. 1, Fall 1972).
11. P. F. Strawson, *Individuals* (New York: Humanities Press, 1963), pp. 97-101.
12. Germain Grisez, *Abortion: the Myths, the Realities, and the Arguments,* New York: Corpus, .971, p. 282.
13. Joseph Fletcher, *Morals and Medicine,* Boston: Beacon Press, 1954, p. 152.
14. Fletcher, *op. cit.,* p. 201.
15. *The Hastings Center Report,* Nov. 1972, p. 3.
16. Terrie Finkbine, "Letters to the Editor," *LOOK* (March 4, 1969), p. 10.
17. Charles Carroll, "Abortion without Ethics," *Abortion and Social Justice,* New York: Sheed & Ward, 1973, p. 258.
18. Ashley Montagu, letter to *New York Times,* March 3, 1967.
19. Simone deBeauvoir, *The Second Sex,* New York: Bantam, 1952, p. 468.
20. Dr. Mace, *op. cit.,* pp. 136-139.
21. Herbert Richardson, "Abortion in Technological Perspective," a paper presented before the National Canadian Conference on Abortion St. Micahel's College, Toronto, May 1972, p. 5.
22. Henry Morgentaler to Lynda Hurst, "Decision is woman's, woman's abortion doctor says," *The Toronto Star,* Nov. 29, 1973, p. E1.
23. Phelan and Maginnis, *The Abortion Handbook for Responsible Women,* Canoga Park, Calif.: Weiss, Day, & Lord, 1969, p. 9.
24. Cf. Grisez, *op. cit.,* p. 275.
25. J. C. Fleming & L. Beebe, "Should Abortion Laws Be Liberalized?", *Good Housekeeping,* (March, 1970), p. 92.

26. Quoted by Jesuit writers in *The Month,* May 1973.
27. Betty Sarvis & Hyman Rodman, *The Abortion Controversy,* New York: Columbia University Press, 1973, p. 25.
28. Dr. Albert W. Liley, "The Foetus in Control of His Environment," *Abortion and Social Justice, op. cit.,* p. 28.
29. Cf. Paul Marx, *The Death Peddlers,* Collegeville, Minnesota: St. John's University Press, 1971, p. 4.
30. Dr. Ken Walker appearing on the Dan Fischer radio show, CKKW Kitchener, Ontario, Nov. 1973.
31. Glanville Williams, "The Legalization of Medical Abortion," *The Eugenics Review,* 56 (April 1964), p. 20.
32. Garrett Hardin, "Abortion and Human Dignity," *The Case for Legalized Abortion Now, op. cit.,* pp. 82-3.
33. *Ibid.*
34. Garrett Hardin, "Abortion — or Compulsory Pregnancy?", *Journal of Marriage and the Family,* 30 (May 1968), p. 249.
35. Kopit and Pilpel, "Abortion and the New York Penal Laws," presented to the New York Civil Liberties Union, April 20, 1965, p. 7.
36. Lorenne M. G. Smith, "Material for Abortion Conference," prepared for the National Conference on Abortion, St. Michael's College, Toronto, May 1972, p. 8.
37. Soren Kierkegaard, *Councluding Unscientific Postscript,* tr. by D. Swenson and W. Lowrie, Princeton: Princeton University Press, 1968, 9th printing, p. 312.

—3—

LEGAL ABORTION: DEMOCRACY OR AUTHORITARIANISM?

Justice Byron White, in his dissent from the January 22, 1973, Supreme Court abortion ruling, described the majority's decision as "an exercise in raw power," "an improvident and extravagant exercise of the power of judicial review." These oft-quoted words raise some very significant philosophical questions.

Was the Supreme Court's decision authoritarianistic? White could find "no constitutional warrant" for its action. Furthermore, Justice William Rehnquist, the other dissenter, stated that the Court's majority had disregarded popular sentiment. He wrote:

> The fact that a majority of States, reflecting after all the majority sentiment in those States, have had restrictions on abortion for at least a century seems to me as strong an indication as there is that the asserted right to an abortion is not . . . fundamental.

Would a national referendum have been a more democratic means of deciding the abortion issue? Pro-life advocates in 1972 abortion referenda polled 63% and 78% of the vote in Michigan and North Dakota. And yet, is popular sentiment necessarily different from the authoritarianism of the court? Are decisions made by nine judges any more authoritarian than decisions made by a national majority? Does popularity justify law? Does democracy render leadership superfluous and authoritarianism optional?

These questions are of fundamental importance and require fundamental thinking if they are to be answered properly. Therefore, an understanding of the presuppositions of democracy and authoritarianism is necessary in order to answer such questions. The following discussion undertakes to explore those presuppositions and then relate them to the abortion issue.

One of the most approachable and illuminating of the great thinkers on the fundamental issues of the polity and the populace is Plato. Because Plato combined a genius for thought with a genius for story-telling, his meaning and imagery continue to be contemporary and refreshing. In his dialogue *Euthyphro,* he raises perhaps the most fundamental of all philosophical questions. But this question would lose some of its significance if presented outside of its context.

Euthyphro is a moralist and theologian who comes to Athens to register a charge of murder against his father. His father had, through cruel negligence, allowed a slave to die. Euthyphro is convinced that his father is guilty of murder and should pay the appropriate penalty. At the entrance to the law courts Euthyphro meets Socrates, who is awaiting trial on the charge of "introducing false divinities and corrupting the youth" of Athens. A conversation ensues between Euthyphro and Socrates. Euthyphro presents himself as a "know-it-all," and Socrates humors himself by engaging to become his pupil. Socrates' first question is, in effect, "How can you be so sure of what is good and what is bad?" Euthyphro answers that charging his father with murder is good and not prosecuting his father would be bad. In other words, what he was doing then was good; the contrary would have been bad.

Undisturbed by the circularity of his argument, Euthyphro is as candid as he is conceited. The discussion continues; Euthyphro states that what is good is so because it is pleasing to the gods; what is bad is so because it is displeasing to the gods. Euthyphro, being a theologian, is confident that he has the inside track on the will of the gods, that his knowledge of what is holy (or good) and what is unholy (or bad) is correct. Socrates then delivers the crucial question:

"Is what is holy holy because the gods approve it, or do they approve it because it is holy?" Euthyphro makes a predictable response, "I do not get your meaning." He is confused by Socrates' question but, as he hurries away, promises to continue the discussion "another time".

Euthyphro can not understand the meaning of Socrates' question because he can not conceive of any other basis for being right than being Euthyphro — as if being right and being Euthyphro were identical.

The contrast between Euthyphro and Socrates is a fascinating instance of a recurring drama in the history of mankind. Euthyphro represents the self-righteous individual who is uninterested in facts, the egoist who insists he is right merely because he needs to be right. Socrates, on the other hand, with his critical and questioning spirit, represents the challenger of egoism. He symbolizes the dissolver of superstition and the seeker of a common basis for truth which all men can share. Euthyphro stands for pride, selfishness, and complacence; Socrates for humility, restraint, and perseverance in the quest for truth. Euthyphro is the authoritarian, Socrates the democrat.

Is something good merely because it is sanctioned, or is it sanctioned because it was good initially? Is a restaurant good because it has been approved by Duncan Hines, or is it approved by Duncan Hines because it was good initially? Does the line of causality run from approval to goodness or from goodness to approval? The answer separates the arbitrary authoritarian from the realist democrat. If what makes a thing good is only that it is sanctioned and approved from outside of itself, then nothing is good in itself, nothing would have its own claim to goodness. This conclusion is equivalent to asserting that a restuarant becomes a good restuarant when the Duncan Hines sticker goes on the window. No realist would hold that the sticker causes the restaurant's goodness. He would argue that the sticker is warranted because the restaurant was good in the first place. The authoritarian holds that the origin of good lies in an external relationship to an observer. When the authoritarian speaks of something as good, he is describing its external relationship to him. The weakness of authoritarianism is that it never gets to reality; it never gets to substance.

Socrates represents the realist. He holds that the gods approve what is holy because it is holy. The goodness of a thing is primary; its being approved or loved is secondary. A man is good not because he is loved but is loved because he is good.

Throughout history, the authoritarian-versus-realist debate has been waged on theological frontiers. Why should the Ten Commandments be obeyed? Are they just merely because God commanded them or did God command them because they are just by their own nature? In the Middle Ages, William of Ockham argued that they are just solely because they are commanded by God. Thomas Aquinas opposed Ockham, saying that good and right have their own inherent character. According to Euthyphro's view laws were just because God commanded them; according to Socrates' view God commanded them because they are just. But if Euthyphro were correct, then, God could command whatever He pleased. If He commanded murder, then murder would be good. If He commanded against murder, murder would be bad. No one could distinguish good from bad unless he first knew God's arbitrary will. Therefore, only the authoritarian should rule. Ordinary people, not being able to divine God's will, should never be allowed a democratic form of government.

Since God, in the authoritarian view, could command anything He pleased, it appears that in issuing His Ten Commandments He was chiefly concerned with manifesting His *power.* On the other hand, if the Commandments are based on a regard and a reverence for what already is good, according to the realist view, His apparent concern in announcing His law was expressing His *love.* Thus, the authoritarian is concerned with power, since what is good is what he arbitrarily decides to be good, while the realist democrat is concerned with love, since he is concerned with serving what he discovers to be good. Authoritarianism, by assuming that ordinary people are incapable of distinguishing good from evil, rejects democracy. Democracy, by presupposing the possibility that ordinary people can discover what is good, rejects authoritarianism.

Democracy, therefore, as the opposite of authoritarianism, is a gamble that ordinary people will have the perception and the moral wisdom to choose the good and reject the bad. But people often forget their responsibility to discover what is good and simply vote thoughtlessly without due regard for the objective state of things.

Christ before Pontius Pilate provides a classic example; a group of people, abdicating their responsibility to perceive the objective situation, became an authoritarian mob. Pilate declared that he saw no fault in Christ. However, since he had no concern for serving justice, he delivered Christ to the crowd.

We remember Pilate as a political coward and a betrayer of justice and goodness. We regard the behavior of the murderous mob as anything but democracy in action. The mob behaved as authoritarians because, disregarding the objectively good and just, they voted merely to satisfy their pleasure.

How, then, shall the abortion issue be resolved? The Supreme Court decision, by basing its judgment on the mother's right to privacy, ignored the reality of the human foetus. Justice Douglas wrote that childbirth "may deprive a woman of her preferred life style and force upon her a radically different and undesired future." A more authoritarian rationale could scarcely be imagined. And yet if the same rationale were used by the majority in a national referendum, that judgment would be equally authoritarianistic.

With the right-to-privacy ruling, the human foetus's right to life is judged to be conferred upon him by his mother. By being unwanted by his mother, the human foetus loses all claim to his existence. What could be a clearer case of arbitrary authoritarianism? The human foetus is nothing until the mother sanctions his existence by wanting or needing him. The human foetus is good only because he is wanted; he is not wanted because he is good. The wish of the mother outweighs the substance of the foetus. The foetus has no intrinsic value, goodness, or dignity. The mother, in conferring value upon him through mere approval, becomes a symbol of power rather than love.

Opponents of abortion develop their discussion from a concern for the objective reality of the foetus which disposes them to accept the proper ordering of things and the rightfulness of creation. Anti-abortionists are realists, because they consider the substantial reality of the human foetus to be good and lovable and consequently more valuable than idea, wish, or convenience. They are democrats because they believe ordinary people to be capable of discovering and affirming the foetus's objective reality and therefore of avoding authoritarian legislation directed against him.

Sacrificing the human foetus for the sake of an ego preference demonstrates a blatant disvaluation of reality, "an exercise in raw power". The human foetus is good because he is a human life struggling by virtue of his own inner dynamism to possess life in a larger measure. By constantly transcending himself in time, in a properly human way, he manifests the common destiny he shares with all men. No man has ever lived who did not once live as a foetus. It is deeply disturbing to think that law now regards the early foetus's right to exist as based no longer on his intrinsic goodness but on someone else's arbitrary decision. Is this not a form of human slavery?

A democratic solution to the abortion issue is possible only if people are enlightened, that is, if they exercise the intellectual vision and moral perspicacity necessary to discover and embrace a world of real values. The authoritarian refusal to revere goodness, and the insistence upon satisfying self prepares for the decay of effective democracy. "It is sad not to see any good in goodness." These words of the Russian author Nikolai Gogol capture the spiritual malaise of modern man. Man has retreated into himself and has demanded the freedom to sever all ties with truths that lie beyond his ego.

When the authoritarian transplants the natural basis for goodness for reality to the ego, he also, by the same stroke, denies the natural basis for his own goodness. If good is only externally and arbitrarily conferred, then the basis for any good, even that of the authoritarian, is undermined. Authoritarianism toward the unborn ultimately invalidates all natural bases upon which human life can be valued as objectively good. At this point no one can enjoy security against arbitrary condemnation. People will live in mutual distrust, ever fearing that the justification of their own existence will suddenly be removed by another as easily as it has been conferred. When democracy yields to authoritarianism, power replaces love. Society can not endure such moral regression.

The human foetus, frail and peaceful, can offer little protest to man's destructive ego. The full burden of wisdom falls upon those who live outside the womb. Theirs is the awesome responsibility to judge wisely the fate of those who must plead their case in silence. The silent plea for life will thunder across man's heart if he only stills his ego to listen to another's truth.

—4—

ABORTION
AND THE
REALIST

ABORTION AND THE REALIST

Pro-abortionists credit themselves with possessing a moral quality that belongs only to the most sober-minded and courageous of thinkers. This is the quality of being realistic — of not shying away from unpleasant facts or ignoring the hard truths of life. They conclude that because women have always found a way to get an abortion, anti-abortion laws are ineffective. They cite the illegal "butchered" abortions that take place under horrendous medical conditions, and prescribe legalized abortion in order to afford abortion-seeking women better protection. The philosophical hypothesis that abortion is morally wrong does not interest them. Facts, not fancies, are their forte. What actually transpires is all they are concerned about.

Realist in the Popular Sense

There are two kinds of people: the idealists and the realists. The former are primarily interested in what people *ought to do* and tend to close their eyes to what people *actually do*. The latter are primarily interested in what people *do* and are not impressed by idealistic theories which suggest the kind of conduct people *ought* to follow. The realists are tuned in to this world of actual events, whereas the idealists are tuned in to a hypothetical world which has not and perhaps never will come into being. Pro-abortionists are called realistic and can be expected to serve people positively; anti-abortionists are labelled idealistic and are of questionable help, at best, to real people with real problems.

In Western history, Thomas More is particularly conspicuous as a moral idealist. He is frequently remembered for advising his Lordship Henry VIII what the kind ought to do. Not being sufficiently realistic or practically sensible, Sir Thomas, in due time, was beheaded by order of the king. During the same period, an audacious, young, Italian philosopher emerged to write of man as he actually was, not as the noble or morally dignified creature he was supposed to be. His name was Nicolo Machiavelli. It is his enduring brand of realism which is personified by today's pro-abortionists.

Realist in the Philosophical Sense

History's judgment of More and Machiavelli, however, takes a surprising turn. Sir Thomas is remembered as the man of courage and sober judgment. Indeed, he is more fondly remembered than the self-righteous and impetuous king who had him beheaded. The Catholic Church saw enough reality in this "idealist" to canonize him in 1935. On the other hand, the "realist" Machiavelli was a complete political failure, because of his having unwisely committed to paper his unscrupulous thinking, and is remembered with disdain and contempt. During the Elizabethan Era, for example, hundreds of references appeared linking Machiavelli with the "Evil One" of the Devil.

Paradoxically, then, the world has recognized something very real about the "idealist" Thomas More and something very unreal about the so-called "realist" Machiavelli. This paradox is resolvable through analysis of *real* and *ideal* as philosophical terms.

If the reality of man is what he does rather than what he ought to do, then it is unrealistic to use anything other than history or a kind of Kinsey report as a basis for morality. Man can never do wrong, because what is right is simply what he does. Consequently, man is not a moral being but merely an historical one. But upon reflection, this position is untenable even to pro-abortionists. They consider it immoral for laws to exist which prohibit or restrict abortions. The pro-abortionists are surely moralists, because they judge that a moral improvement results wherever abortion laws are relaxed. So-called "realist" pro-abortionists are themselves idealists, since they are trying to make "what is" coincide with what they think "ought to be".

Truthfully, there is no reality without the coincidence of "what is" with "what ought to be". Unless the actual (what is) is in some way an actualization of an ideal (what ought to be), nothing really happens. The term "realist" is a misnomer. It should be "actualist". The actual and the ideal are indispensable components of the real. The "poor player who struts and frets his hour upon the stage" is less real as a player than Olivier or Gielgud. But he is not less actual. The performer who scratches and hacks at his violin, producing no music, is not performing as a real violinist. He may be a real fraud, but he is not a real violinist because he is not actualizing the ideals of violin playing. The imposter violinist may evoke calls from the audience to "bring on the real violinist."

A man is not a fully real man simply because he actually exists. Man expresses his reality to the degree that he actualizes in his life certain ideals or principles which are consonant with his nature. Man's reality, his authenticity, his manhood, is not automatically received, but must be chosen and earned through struggle. Napoleon's famous remark about Goethe, "Here is a man," was made not to indicate the species membership of the poet, but to call attention to the high degree of human reality which Goethe manifested. The remark that "man *alive* is the glory of God," carries a similar implication.

The contrast between the actual and the ideal, in man, is clearly evinced by William Hazlitt's observation:

> Man is the only animal that laughs and weeps; for he is the only animal that is struck with the difference between what things are, and what they ought to be.

Realists, True and False

St. Thomas More was a true realist because he knew that reality is richer than the mere actual, present-at-hand. He knew of destiny, and moral order, and principles by which the actual and the ideal fused into the real. His vision extended beyond the present, the actual, the factual. Machiavelli was a false realist. His vision was not broad enough to see more than one component of reality. He was a pessimist, because, unable to recognize the truth of ideals, he saw no sense or substance to man, no reality, ultimate value or hope.

The pro-abortionists are likewise unrealistic. They take the actual, the existing situation, and think that it alone is real. The anti-abortionists are realistic, because they know that the reality of man begins to emerge only when the actually existing situation begins to move toward what is good for it, its ideal.

Michelangelo never saw a block of marble as simply a block of marble. Being more than an accountant, he was able to breathe reality into things. He envisioned the beautiful art form his raw material could be. His work as an artist consisted in fusing the actual marble with the ideal form he had in his mind.

Realism and Correctibility

Two common English words which denote the fusion of the actual with an ideal are 'improvable' and 'correctible'. 'Improvable' refers to something's readiness to be made better than it now is. This represents the movement of the actual toward an ideal. 'Correctible' means 'able to be made right'. This presupposes a distinction between *incorrect* (what it was before being corrected), and *correct* (what it is after being corrected). The word 'correctible' indicates the possibility of the fusion of the actual with an ideal. People concerned with the 'improvable' and 'correctible' are not starry-eyed idealists but objective realists.

Anti-abortionists, being realistic, locate their solutions within the realm of the possible. Therefore, they are concerned with what is correctible. The economic, social or personal plight of the distressed pregnant mother is at least theoretically correctible. But abortion, being irrevocable, is not correctible even in theory. Once the baby is lost, he is lost forever. Abortion is non-correctible, whereas the problems that give rise to abortions, in most cases, are correctible. If a child is not wanted by his natural mother, adoption resolves the problem. If economic, emotional, physical, or social difficulties surround a pregnancy, the appropriate agencies of help could resolve these difficulties without abortion. There are many ways in which all or nearly all the difficulties which attend a pregnancy are resolvable apart from the irrevocable act of aborting. Abortion is an unrealistic solution to a problem because the aborted foetus loses all his reality, without any possibility of its recovery.

The realist deals with what is correctible and is concerned about getting the actual (what is, or how it is at the moment) and the ideal (what ought to be, or how it should be) to coincide. For this reason the anti-abortionist is the true realist. The pro-abortionist deals with only the actual and seeks to resolve difficulties by either tolerating existing conditions (since abortion is ineradicable) or destroying them (aborting the unwanted foetus).

Realism and Love

The true realist, who believes that there is more to reality than anyone can actually see at any given moment, lives and works by the conviction that man is improvable and that his situation is correctible. He understands that all is not yet given, because reality awaits the active response of man's love — that indispensable nourishment by which man slowly coaxes fellow man toward completion. In the words of author, anthropologist Loren Eiseley:

> The truth is that if man at heart were not a tender creature toward his kind, a loving creature in a peculiarly special way, he would long since have left his bones to the wild dogs that roved the African grasslands where he first essayed the great adventure of becoming human.

Love, born of the realistic instinct that man can grow and advance, has allowed the human race to continue, develop, and sometimes even prosper. The great adventure of becoming more really human, of actualizing more and more of the ideals of manhood, could not take place without vision and love. Actual man may still be a long way from the fully real man, but he would perish without envisioning, in some way, the distant goal, and loving the enduring struggle which spans the treacherous gap between the actual and the ideal.

—5—

DOES WONDER EVER CEASE?

By far the most remarkable transplant in modern medicine is the one which removes wonder from the bosom of nature and installs it in the heart of technology. Conception, once considered a natural miracle, is now commonly called an 'accident' or a 'mistake', while synthesized medicinals are frequently labelled 'wonder drugs' or 'wonder pills'. Prophets and holy men, who once commanded a natural, reverential awe, have been superannuated by wonder-working technicians. Nature, in being conquered by science, has supposedly surrendered most of the long-guarded secrets which formerly gave her an aura of mystery and wondrous allure. Technology, nature's successor, is progressing at such a dizzying pace it is creating the impression that nature is antiquated.

Today the 'Natural Look' is a technological achievement. 'Natural Freshness' is mass produced in spray cans. Butter cannot be distinguished from margarine by the embarrassed Mother Nature of a TV commercial. A man of vitality is flatteringly told he 'looks like a million dollars'. The wonder in 'Mr. Wonderful' has been replaced by computerized matching. Life is no longer 'onederful', quipped Victor Borge; thanks to inflation it is now 'twoderful'.

As a result of the wonder transplant, people have become more enchanted with man's technological achievement than with man himself. This strange, inverted state or affairs is all too apparent in pro-abortion thinking. At a 1972 Toronto abortion conference one of the chief participants appraised the early human embryo as a mere 'dot'. The purpose of this blase, wonderless description was to justify abortion.

It is ironic that this statement was made by a philosopher. Wonder has been the inspiration and guiding star of philosophy since its inception. The contemporary technician-philosopher bargains away wonder for technological control. Life becomes a mechanism that society may permit, rather than a marvel that man should revere. Philosophy begins in wonder but it stops in willfulness.

So intimate to man is wonder that it is the natural form of his involuntary praise of creation. And yet, wonder is a paradox. It bestows comfort but incites curiosity. A starry night inspires wonder because its cause, being, and beauty offer peace to man's restless heart but surpass the narrow limitations of his questioning mind.

The human embryo is a profound paradox. Though barely visible to the naked eye, he embodies a genetic blueprint of such complexity that 18 to 25 years of time are required for its reading.

If, as Wordsworth wrote, "The child is father of the man," the embryo is still more remarkable. He is the father of the father of man. He is time compressed in a moment. His death is the loss of each future development that would have been. Because he is least activated, he has the most to gain or lose. He has crossed over the treshhold from nothingness, an accomplishment which required all the eons of evolution. His cosmogenesis is but a fraction away from completion while his ontogeny has just begun. He is a paradox of paradoxes and a wonder of wonders.

Dr. H.M.I. Liley was able to observe, through a sort of closed-circuit x-ray television set, the unborn child during the middle weeks of pregnancy. She describes him reverently, fully sensitive to the natural wonder of prenatal life.

> The head, housing the miraculous brain, is quite large in proportion to the remainder of the body, and the limbs are still relatively small. Within his watery world, however, he is quite beautiful, perfect in his fashion, active and graceful. He is neither a witless tadpole, as some have conceived him to be in the past, but rather a tiny human being, as independent as though he were lying in a crib with a blanket wrapped around him instead of his mother *(Modern Motherhood,* pp. 26-7).

In 1959, Dr. Paul Rockwell was privileged to observe in the natural state what he believed to be the smallest human being ever seen. While giving the anesthetic during an operation to remove a tubal pregnancy of two months, he was handed the transparent, intact embryo sac containing a human male still attached to the wall by the umbilical cord. The tiny boy, only one-third inch long, was swimming quite vigorously in the amniotic fluid. Dr. Rockwell described this perfectly developed tiny human as follows:

> The baby was extremely alive and swam about the sac approximately one time per second with a natural swimmer's stroke. This tiny human did not look at all like the photos and drawings of 'embryos' which I have seen, nor did it look like the few embryos I have been

able to observe since then, obviously because this one was alive.

"The world will never starve for want of wonders," Chesterton wrote, "but only for want of wonder." Wonders never cease, but it is all too easy for man to cease to wonder. The stars lost their divinity, it has been remarked, with the development of astronomy. With the dawn of the science of fetology, is man's wonder for the human foetus beginning to wane? It has also been said that wonder is the result of novelty's being met by ignorance. But natural wonders are as inexhaustible as things of beauty are joys forever. Wonder would never cease if only the penetrating eye of the scientist were joined by the receptive heart of the poet. The scientist may know more about things, but the poet still knows them better. If people could only look upon the human foetus with the poetic feeling Keats experienced on first looking into Chapman's Homer, man's wonder for the foetus would never cease.

> Then I felt some watcher of the skies
> When a new planet swims into his ken;
> Or like stout Cortez when with eagle eyes
> He star'd at the Pacific — and all his men
> Look'd at each other with a wild surmise —
> Silent, upon a peak in Darien.

"Beauty is mysterious as well as terrible," wrote Dostoevsky. "God and the Devil are fighting there, and the battlefield is the human heart."

—6—

CONSCIENCE AND CIVIL LAWS

A man must act according to his conscience, but . . . . And that is just the trouble with moral platitudes — there is always a "but". Vigorous statements that redound with courage and determination lose their idealistic, nothing-can-stop-me-now tone when they meet complex reality head-on. A man must act according to his conscience, but so may society constrain him according to its collective conscience. A man is free to follow the dictates of his conscience only as long as society grants him permission to do so. He may conscientiously act contrary to law, but society retains the right to revoke his civil liberties.

It is simply one of those hard facts of life that individual conscience and collective conscience often differ. Civil law is the expression of collective conscience; individual free choice is the expression of individual conscience. Where there is disharmony between the two, an individual may oppose the law, but he usually does so with the aim of replacing the law with a better one and not of abolishing it altogether so that in the absence of law his individual conscience can express itself without constraint. This reforming rather than abolishing attitude is the only realistic one where the law in question concerns the life and health of citizens, and the stability of society.

The complete absence of civil law is equivalent to social anarchy; the complete absence of individual free choice is totalitarianism. What is indispensable for democracy is the ever-present opportunity for individual consciences to guide the formation of better civil laws.

Dr. Henry Morgentaler together with his intellectual supporters have recently stirred a conscience controversy because they have stated that the current Canadian abortion law fails to honor the consciences of many thousands of women (especially Quebec women) who believe that abortion for them is a morally righteous choice. While it is well known that a good conscience will break a bad law, it is equally well known that a bad conscience will break a good law. What Canada needs more than conscience replacing law is a *good* abortion law, that is, one which would afford maximum protection to all concerned — foetus, pregnant woman, her future progeny, and society in general.

The argument that the current abortion law should be abolished entirely so that women can procure without civil constraint a conscientious abortion, fails to take cognizance of both the reason for law as well as the nature of conscience. Law exists to protect the members of society and to provide for a stable social order. Conscience is so involved in the subjective, and so prone to erroneous judgment, that it can be malformed, uninformed, lax, scrupulous, numb, or nonfunctional. To abandon law and the protective and stabilizing values it represents for the unconstrained expression of consciences that can be misshappen in every conceivable way is to invite social anarchy.

The deeper significance of the statement, "A man must act according to his conscience", is religious rather than political. No one is capable of judging the conscience of another. As Lammenais put it, "Conscience is a sacred sanctuary where God alone may enter as judge".

No magistrate can assess the conscience of any citizen. And yet there must be magistrates, and citizens must stand trial. Social justice and the preservation of the social order demand this. What must be judged by man, then, is the observance or the non-observance of the law — something external and tangible. Conscience is important for man as he stands before God, not as he stands before the civil authorities.

It would be impossible, therefore, to do justice to a "conscientious abortion act" that would replace an abortion law since no one, save God, could read anyone else's conscience. A person would have little difficulty in dissimulating his own conscience to achieve an immoral end and no reliable means could be made available to disclose such dissimulation. Society would be at the mercy of its least honorable members and its most honorable members would be helpless to expose such duplicity.

A man must act according to his conscience, but he must contend with and have a healthy respect for society's existing laws. Furthermore, since God is his judge, he bears the obligation of forming his conscience in the face of that consideration and not subjectively according to the desires of his ego. Conscience, far from suggesting moral autonomy and a simple way of resolving moral issues, implies complex responsibilities that include the societal as well as the divine.

II

WHOSE CHILD IS THIS?

"If there had been no womb in which we first grew as embryos, language would not be possible; and if there had been no birth, language would not be necessary."

—Rollo May

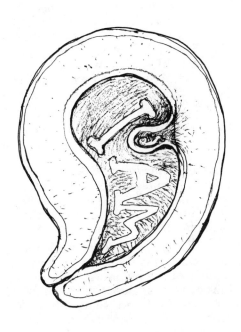

—7—

THE MERCHANTS
OF
CALUMNY

In all of English literature, perhaps the most dramatic and devastating argument against prejudice is that given by Shylock in *The Merchant of Venice:*

> ...I am a Jew. Hath not a Jew eyes? hath not a Jew hands, organs, dimensions, senses, affections, passions? fed with the same food, hurt with the same weapons, subject to the same diseases, healed by the same means, warmed and cooled by the same winter and summer, as a Christian is? If you prick us, do we not bleed? if you tickle us, do we not laugh? if you poison us, do we not die? and if you wrong us, shall we not revenge? if we are like you in the rest, we will resemble you in that.[1]

There can be no retort to Shylock's statement. One must either recognize the facts and agree that Shylock is human and deserving of treatment equal to Christians, or ignore the facts and walk away. The Jew's self-defense is too fundamental to be undercut. He wisely avoids sophisticated reasons, academic distinctions, and intellectual subtleties that could render his argument suspect, weak, or unclear. His self-defense is really a self-description and in describing the elementary fact he makes his case irrefutable.

Taking the fundamental and forthright approach of Shylock, can we raise a convincing argument in defense of the humanity of the human foetus and his right to equal protection to that of adults? Substituting 'human foetus' for 'Jew' and 'adult' for Christian', can we use Shylock's argument to defend the human unborn against his detractors — the merchants of calumny?

1) "I am a human foetus:

In his article "The Humanity of the Unborn Child," pediatrician Eugene Diamond writes:

> To consider the fetus not to be a separate person but merely a part of the mother has not been tenable since

the sixteenth century when Arantius showed that the maternal and fetal circulations were separate — neither continuous nor contiguous.[2]

Medical evidence[3] is contrary to the unscientific views of Justice Holmes, who once declared that the unborn child is "a part of its mother."[4] It shows conclusively that the foetus is a human being in its own right "with its separate principle of growth and development, with its separate nervous system and blood circulation, with its own skeleton and musculature, its brain and heart and vital organs."[5]

Genetics clearly establishes the human foetus as a member of the human race by recognizing that his 23 pairs of chromosomes per somatic cell are derived equally from a human mother and a human father. Fetology establishes the selfhood of the human foetus by tracing his growth and development from a single cell which belongs neither to mother nor father. Dr. H. M. I. Liley writes:

He (the unborn baby) has his own space capsule, the amniotic sac. He has his own lifeline, the umbilical cord, and he has his own root system, the placenta. These all belong to the baby himself, not to his mother. They are all developed from his original cell.[6]

The selfhood of the human foetus is further corroborated by electrocardiographic (ECG) readings of his heart beat at 7½ weeks[7] and electroencephalographic (EEG) recordings of his brain waves at 6 weeks.[8]

2) ...Hath not a human foetus eyes?

His eyes begin to form at 19 days. By 8½ weeks the eyelids become sensitive to touch. If the eyelid is stroked, the child will squint.[9] Rugh and Shettles describe the foetus after 8 weeks as having "a human face with eyelids half closed as they are in someone who is about to fall asleep."[10] During the fifth month the hair of his eyebrows begins to grow and a fringe of eyelashes appears.

In the sixth month his eyelids will open and close. His eyes will look up, down, and sideways. The iris diaphragm will contract or dilate to admit the proper light intensity. Dr. Albert Liley contends that the child may perceive light through the abdominal wall of his mother.[11]

3) ...hath not a human foetus hands, organs, dimensions, senses, affections, passions?

The hands, with fingers and thumbs, are recognizable by the seventh week of fetal life.[12] The lines in the hands (and feet), which will remain a distinctive feature throughout the life of the individual, are engraved at 8 weeks.[13] At 8½ weeks the palms of the hands become sensitive to touch. If the palm of the foetus is touched, his fingers will close to a small fist.[14] The child's grip at 16 weeks is quite strong. At this time he is able to maintain his grasp on an object, such as a slender rod, while that object is being moved up and down or slightly away from him.[15]

All the organ systems are present in the human foetus by 8 weeks.[16] In the ninth and tenth weeks, if the child's forehead is touched, he may turn his head away from the stimulus and pucker up his brow and frown. By the twelfth week, his organs, dimensions, senses, affections, and passions are present and operative.

> By the end of the first trimester (twelfth week), the fetus is a sentient moving being. We need not pause to speculate as to the nature of his psychic attributes but we may assume that the organization of psycho-somatic self is now well underway.[17]

4) . . .fed with the same food,

In Shakespearian England, as scholars have pointed out, the segregated Jew did not dine in the company of the Christian. Moreover, in accordance with his Jewish tradition, his diet was markedly different from that of the Christian. The human foetus and his mother, on the other hand, are quite literally fed with the same food.

The taste buds and the salivary and digestive glands develop in the foetus during the third month. At this time the baby is able to swallow and utilize amniotic fluid.[18] Although the blood of the mother and her child do not mix during foetal development, the child receives oxygen and food from his mother through placental attachment, "much as he receives food from her after he is born."[19]

When a child *in utero* fails to receive adequate nourishment, it is possible to correct this problem by injecting supplementary nutrients directly into the amniotic fluid which he normally swallows in the amount of 250-700 cc a day. One doctor states, "We well may be able to offer the child that is starving because of a placental defect a nipple to use before birth."[20]

5) . . .hurt with the same weapons,

In an early 1972 interview, a California doctor who performed abortions was asked: "Doctor, what does the aborted baby feel while it's dying?" The doctor answered, "Oh, I think that depends on your philosophy." Furthermore, he stated that the question was not an important one.[21]

To Dr. Albert W. Liley, pre-eminent fetologist of New Zealand, the crucially important question of foetal pain can be answered on the basis of objective evidence. In 1963 Dr. Liley developed the first surgical technique for administering intrauterine blood transfusions to the foetus.[22] According to Dr. Liley, the foetus feels pain as early as three months. In offering instructions for carrying out the surgical technique of foetal blood transfusions, he advises his colleagues to take into serious consideration this fact of foetal pain. During the actual surgical procedure the child must be sedated and given pain-relieving medication. Dr. H.M.I. Liley, wife and research assistant to Dr. Albert Liley and a distinguished fetologist and pediatrician in her own right, remarks in her well-known book *Modern Motherhood:*

> When doctors first began invading the sanctuary of the womb, they did not know that the unborn baby would react to pain in the same fashion as a child would. But they soon learned that he would. By no means a 'vegetable' as he has so often been pictured, the unborn knows perfectly well when he has been hurt, and he will protest it just as violently as would a baby lying in a crib.[23]

In reference to aborting a 12-week-old foetus by the method of dilatation and curettage (D & C, in which the neck of the womb is dilated and the foetus removed in pieces after the womb has been scraped by a sharp instrument called a curette), Dr. Eugene Diamond states:

> When this procedure is done, there is little doubt that the foetus, in fact, feels what is done to it.[24]

In the words of physician Gino Papola, "The curette will become mightier than the sword."[25]

The weaponry used against the unborn — curette, suction, and salt, together with the starvation and suffocation which follow a hysterotomy — is fatal for physiological reasons alone. If an adult were similarly assaulted, he would succumb for the same medical reasons as does the aborted foetus.

6) ...subject to the same diseases,

Dr. H.M.I. Liley writes:

> No problem in fetal health or disease can any longer be considered in isolation. At the very least two people are involved, the mother and her child.[26]

The most convenient way in which the physician may diagnose the condition of the foetus is from an analysis of the amniotic fluid which surrounds the unborn child. In observing the color, turbidity and volume of the amniotic fluid, or the enzymes and other chemicals contained therein, he is able to diagnose a long list of foetal diseases.[27] In addition, the electrocardiogram of the unborn and the analysis of his heart sounds through phonocardiography is helpful to the diagnostician.

In Ashley Montagu's book, *Life before Birth,* the author lists some of the diseases which may afflict the unborn child. The list includes pneumonia, scarlet fever, typhoid, streptococcal infections, rheumatic fever, listeriosis, syphilis, malaria, virus diseases, tuberculosis, viral hepatitis, and others. All these diseases can be transmitted from the pregnant mother to her unborn child.[28]

7) ...healed by the same means,

Dr. Liley's technique of intrauterine blood transfusion has been mentioned. Perhaps the most famous case involving a blood transfusion given to the unborn foetus occurred in 1964. Because of certain religious beliefs, a pregnant woman refused to allow her unborn to undergo a blood transfusion. The child, because of an Rh problem in his blood, vitally needed this particular operation. The case went to court. The judge ruled that the unborn's right to survival was a value which out-weighed the mother's right to practice her religious beliefs in this manner.[29]

Analysis of the amniotic fluid surrounding the unborn has led to diagnoses of the adrenogenital syndrome, hemolytic anemia, adrenal insufficiency, congenital hyperuricemia, and glycogen storage disease. Some of these maladies can now be treated before birth;[30] it is expected that someday all of them can be.

There are ways in which nature heals an injured foetus without medical assistance. If the child sustains a fractured limb when his mother falls, the limb will heal naturally. Even a gunshot wound (incurred at three months) will heal naturally, and only a scar will remain at the time of birth.[31]

8) ...warmed and cooled by the same winter and summer as an adult is?

The unborn is directly affected by temperature extremes, or changes.[32]

When the body is colder than normal, the brain needs less oxygen than normal, because metabolism is retarded and oxygen is circulated in the blood stream at a slower rate. When a patient faces a lengthy operation, it is sometimes medically expedient to cool his body so as to prevent possibly harmful effects to the brain from large doses of anaesthesia.

Drs. F. Wilson and C.B. Sedzmir have reported the case of a woman, 32 weeks pregnant, who had been cooled in preparation for surgery. As her body temperature was being reduced, the heartbeat of her unborn child dropped from 160 to 85 beats per minute. Furthermore, when trimethaphan was injected into the woman to provide a relatively bloodless field for surgery, the foetus protested by kicking rather furiously. The doctors conjectured that the kicking was brought on by anoxia (lack of oxygen) induced in the child by the drug injection. In another case, a patient's temperature was cooled to 86 degrees F. prior to her operation. At the same time her 24-week unborn child's hearbeat fell from 180 beats per minute to 120.[33] In both cases, after the mother's temperature had returned to normal, the child's metabolic and circulatory rates likewise returned to normal.

9) . . .If you prick us do we not bleed?

Blood cells begin to appear at about 17 days. The heart commences development at 18 days, and although this figure is given as the normal time for such development, Marcel and Exchaquet attest to observing contractions of the heart as early as two weeks.[34]

At 30 days the heart is beating regularly 65 times a minute[35] and pumping blood cells through a closed circulatory system.[36] At 5½ weeks it is functionally complete and, in general configuration, is essentially similar to that of an adult heart.[37]

By the seventh week of life, the liver is manufacturing red blood cells and the kidney is eliminating uric acid from the blood.[38] Straus et al. have shown that the electrocardiogram of a 7½ week foetus demonstrates the existence of a functionally complete cardiac system.[39]

The blood which the unborn sheds in abortion is his own, its type (antigens and antibodies) having been determined genetically at conception.

10) . . .If you tickle us do we not laugh?

Doctor Andre Hellegers writes:

> If we tickle the baby's nose, he will flex his head backwards away from the stimulus.[40]

About the end of the twelfth week the vocal cords of the unborn are completed. The child, however, is unable to cry (or laugh), primarily because his voice cannot be activated in the absence of air.[41]

Dr. H.M.I. Liley relates an incident which occurred after an air bubble had been injected into an 8-month unborn baby's amniotic sac for the purpose of locating the placenta on x-ray. When the air bubble happened to cover the child's face, the child inhaled, allowing his vocal cords to become operative, and produced a cry which was clearly audible to all those present, including the physician and the technical assistants. The mother later reported to the doctor that the air bubble kept moving over the baby's face whenever she lay down to sleep, allowing the child to cry so loudly that both she and her husband were kept awake.[42]

11) . . .if you poison us do we not die?

Dr. Paul Marx describes abortion induced by saline poisoning:

> Then a long needle is skillfully used to puncture the abdomen and uterus — skillfully, because the doctor may hit the brain or body of the baby and draw blood whereas he wishes to withdraw a considerable amount of amniotic fluid. When the fluid has been withdrawn, the abortionist next infuses in its place an equal volume of hypertonic saline, a strong, sterile, salt-water solution which, in effect, pickles the baby alive. He may thrash about for some time but soon becomes still in death. The mother will to into labor and deliver her dead child, on the average, about twenty-four hours after amnio-infusion, though the period may range from three hours to three days — or even several weeks.[43]

There is scientific evidence that the unborn child is as suscentible to poisoning as the rest of the population is.[44] Lead, mercury, arsenic, copper, phosphorous, bromide, iodide, potassium chlorate, and strontium are just a few of the many inorganic poisons which can reach the child through his mother's body.[45]

Dr. P. Bernhard in 1949 and Dr. J.M. O'Lane and Dr. J.R. Zabriskie in 1963 found, as as result of their extensive studies, a strong index of correlation between smoking during pregnancy and spontaneous abortion and prematurity[46] (prematurity is the leading cause of death in early infancy).[47]

12) . . .and if you wrong us, shall we not revenge? if we are like you in the rest, we will resemble you in that."

It is written in the Talmud that, "Whosoever sheds the blood of man within man, his blood shall be shed."[48]

Professor Ian Donald of Glasgow University, referring to the deaths of 15 mothers as a result of the 20,000 legal abortions in England in 1969, states:

> We can look forward to this (legal abortion) being the dominant cause of death to young women.[49]

The Royal College of Obstetrics and Gynaecology, in *Abortion Act (1967),* a inquiry into the effects of the first year of England's permissive law, states:

> Eight maternal deaths occurred in relation to 27,331 terminations of pregnancy during the year 1968-9. This gives a mortality rate of 0.3 per thousand, which is higher than the maternal mortality rate (including abortions, criminal or otherwise) for all pregnancies in England and Wales at the comparable time. A statement issued by the Secretary of State to Parliament on 4 February 1970 reveals a similar state of affairs in respect

46

of about 54,000 induced abortions notified from all sources during 1969; among these there were 15 maternal deaths.[50]

In a documented report prepared in January 1971, for presentation before the Minnesota State Legislature, legal-abortion mortality rates were compared to the maternal mortality rates per births. The maternal mortality rate for the state of Minnesota was established by Rosenfield et al.[51] at 14 per 100,000 live births. In countries having a history of legal abortions, the maternal mortality rate was 66 per 100,000 legal abortions in Finland, 41.4 in Denmark, 39.2 in Sweden, and 39.2 in Great Britain.[52]

On the basis of the mortality rates for mothers undergoing legal abortions in various countries, the following conclusion was reached by the American College of Obstetrics and Gynecology:

> The inherent risks of a therapeutic abortion are serious and may be life-threatening; this fact should be fully appreciated by both the medical profession and the public. In nations where abortion may be obtained on demand, a considerable morbidity and mortality have reported.[53]

Apart from mortality figures, non-fatal medical complications (morbidity) arising from induced abortions have been documented, indicating the grave risks to health and fertility a woman assumes in undergoing an abortion.

Dr. Stallworthy et al. reported a survey of 1,182 legal abortions in one teaching hospital in England. The report showed that nearly 17% of the patients lost more than 500 ml. of blood and 9.5% required transfusion. In addition, cervical lacerations occurred in 4.2%, and the uterus was perforated in 1.2%. Emergency laparotomy was required 6 times and hysterectomy was twice necessary to save life. In 27% of the patients pyrexia (high fever) of 38°C or more persisted for longer than 24 hours. Fourteen patients suffered peritonitis.[54]

"It is disquieting," wrote the doctors, "that postabortal infection, which is one of the common causes of death after criminal abortion, should have occurred in 27% of this series."[55]

The Stallworthy report was especially disturbing since it showed almost identical results with those reported by Sood.[56]

Dr. Droegemuller, reporting on Colorado's first-year experience with legal abortion, reported that 8 out of every 100 women required blood transfusions after being aborted.[57]

The incidence of major hemorrhaging following legal abortion was reported in Russia as 14.2%[58] (D & C), Great Britain 21%[59] (all methods of inducing abortion, and Sweden 3 to 7.8% (saline).

In Japan, the 1969 survey of the office of the Prime Minister reported the following complications resulting from induced abortion: 9% sterility after three years, 14% habitual spontaneous abortion, 4% extra-uterine pregnancies, 17% menstrual irregularities, 20% abdominal pains, 19% dizziness, 27% headache, 3% frigidity, 13% exhaustion, and 3% neurosis.[61]

The Nagoya survey by the Women's Associations reported 59% were severely troubled with adverse after-effects or were in poorer health following abortions. In the Mainichi survey in 1969, 18% complained of being physically unwell after one abortion; 27% after two, 40% after three, and 51% after four.[62]

The Swedish experience with legal abortion is well documented. Perhaps the most thorough follow-up study has been done by Dr. Martin Ekblad. Dr. Ekblad studied 479 women at the time of their abortion and again 2-3½ years later. He found that 10% felt the operation unpleasant, 14% had mild self-reproach, 11% suffered serious self-reproach and self-regret, and 1% had gross psychiatric breakdowns.[63]

A study in Poland has shown a 14% decrease in sexual libido 4 to 5 years after abortion;[64] while the Czechs have reported decrease in libido in 33% of patients 9 months after the abortion.[65]

It has been said that, "You can drag a baby out of the uterus but you cannot wipe it out of the mind."[66] According to certain psychologists and psychiatrists, the feminine principle is one of receiving, keeping, and nourishing.[67] Although the pregnant woman may initially deny her unborn child, once she admits she is pregnant (and she must do this to undergo an abortion) she feels an unconscious attachment to him. Because of this, many women feel that part of themselves is lost through abortion.[68]

The psychiatrist Karl Stern states that it is not infrequent that women who have had abortions break down with a serious depression or even psychosis when the time arrives when they would have given birth to their child. What is remarkable about this, notes Stern, is that the patient may very well be unaware of the due date, or even indifferent to the moral dimension of abortion. Her profound reaction of loss is a natural reaction to the birth which did not take place.[69]

A world Health Organization group of scientists have concluded that:

> There is not doubt that the termination of pregnancy may precipitate a serious psychoneurotic or even psychotic reaction in a susceptible individual.[70]

Apart from the death brought to the unborn, and the mortality or morbidity suffered by the mother as a result of abortion, there are also serious dangers to subsequent children of aborted mothers.

Fourteen years after legalizing abortion, Hungary reported a 5% increase in premature babies.[71] In addition, because of birth injury, post-natal asphyxia, and atelectasis (collapsing of the lungs) which are leading causes of death in premature infants, Hungary's infancy mortality rate was 1,278.2 per 100,000 live births compared to 549.4 per 100,000 for the U.S.[72] Following legalized abortion on request, the perinatal mortality rate in Hungary doubled!

The frequency of spontaneous abortions (miscarriages) in women who have undergone legal abortions has been reported as 30 to 40% higher than in cases where women had not been aborted.[73] Furthermore, the incidence of foetal death during pregnancy is twice as great for a woman who has had an abortion compared to those who have not.[74] Dr. Demetrios Kelaris, whom U.S. Air Force officials in Athens have described as the best obstetrician and gynecologist in Greece, says that one of his country's biggest gynecological and obstetrical problems is women's inability to retain pregnancies because of previous and sometimes multiple abortions.[75]

Findings such as these have led one authority to conclude:

> Induced abortion plays an important role in the development of a subsequent child ... the impact of premature birth on infant mortality and of the mental and physical development of the child is connected with the frequency of abortions.[76]

Dr. Alfred Kotasek of Czechoslovakia corroborates this conclusion:

> Furthermore, as noticed recently, a high incidence of cervical incompetence results from interruption of pregnancy that raises the number of spontaneous abortions to 30-40%. These legal abortions affect subsequent pregnancies and births. We rather often observe complications such as rigidity of the os, placenta adherens, placenta accreta, and atony of the uterus.[77]

Professional researchers Margaret and Arthur Wynn draw a similar conclusion:

> The complications of subsequent pregnancy resulting in children being born handicapped in greater or less degree could be the most expensive consequence of induced abortion for society and most grievous for the individual and her family.
>
> ...The number of abortions aimed at reducing the number of handicapped children is, however, very small compared with the number of abortions liable to increase the prevalence of handicap.[78]

Just as Shylock, the Jew, cannot be discriminated against with impunity, the human foetus cannot be aborted without grave consequences to his mother, her future progeny, the medical profession, and the rest of society. The merchants of claumny who banalize the human foetus and suppress information about the medical risks of abortion are bargaining for their own pound of flesh.

Some people strongly desire to believe that the human foetus is not human and that abortion does not give rise to frequent and serious complications. They prefer that the world they want to exist should serve them rather than that they themselves should serve the world that does exist. They make their own desires the object of their faith and thus become incredulous of the truths which conflict with these desires. The punishment for such egoism is blindness.

Perhaps the essence of prejudice is the fear of accepting what is different. But prejudice against the human foetus takes an ironic twist. We all contain the unborn. We are the unborn. The abortionist is the inverse of Narcissus. He hates his own repeated image. He has no memory. He has no ontogeny. The human foetus tells him how small he must be. In rejecting his own smallness, he lashes out against the unborn. The essential paradox of man is that to accept one's smallness requires greatness.

In accepting his smallness, his finitude, his fallibility, man honors a truth and thereby acknowledges the universe. When he insists upon his own perfection, emancipated forever from any attachment or resemblance to the humble foetus, he confesses his vanity.

Inseparable from a fear of finitude is a fear of death. If man grows from a single cell, what fortress in this world can ever be a safeguard against his destruction? If man's life beings in the shadow of nothingness, that shadow must remain to lurk behind his every heartbeat.

As he came forth from his mother's womb, so again shall he depart, naked as he came, having nothing from his labor that he can carry in his hand.[79]

* * * * * * * * *

FOOTNOTES

1. Shakespeare, *The Merchant of Venice.* Act III, Scene i.
2. Eugene Diamond, "The Humanity of the Unborn." *Catholic Lawyer.* Spring, 1971, p. 174.
3. *Dietrich v. Northhampton.* 138 Mass. 14, 52 *Am. Rep.* 242 (1884).

4. That is to say the current findings in embryology, fetology, perinatology, and all of the biology.
5. David Granfield, *The Abortion Decision*. Doubleday, 1971, p. 23.
6. Day & Liley, *The Secret World of a Baby*. Random House, 1968.
7. Reuben Straus et al., "Direct Electroencephalographic Recording of a Twenty-Three Millimeter Human Embryo," *The American Journal of Cardiology.*" Sept. 1961, pp. 443-47.
8. J.W. Still, *Washington Acad. Sci.* 59:46, 1969.
9. Davenport Hooker, *The Prenatal Origin of Behavior,* Univ. of Kansas Press, 1952. G.L. Flanagan, *The First Nine Months of Life.* Simon & Schuster, 1962.
10. Robert Rugh & Landrum Shettles with R.E. Einhorn. *From Conception to Birth: The Drama of Life's Beginnings.* Harper & Row, 1971, p. 71.
11. Albert W. Liley, "Auckland MD to Measure Light and Sound Inside Uterus," *Medical Tribune Report,* May 26, 1969.
12. Bradley, *Human Embryology.* Third Edition. Ch. 9. McGraw-Hill, 1968
13. Arnold Gesell, *The Embryology of Behavior* Chs. 5-6, 10. Harper & Row, 1945.
14. Davenport Hooker, "Early Human Fetal Behavior with a Preliminary Note on Double Simultaneous Fetal Stimulation." *Proceedings of the Association for Research in Nervous and Mental Disease.* Williams & Wilkins, 1954.
15. Cf. photograph in G.L. Flanagan, *op. cit.* p. 98. (Photograph by the courtesy of Hooker & Humphrey).
16. Dr. & Mrs. J.C. Willke, *Handbook on Abortion,* Hiltz, 1971, p. 21.
17. Arnold Gesell, *op. cit.* p. 65.
18. Carl Wood, "Weightlessness: Its Implications for the Human Fetus." *J. Obstetrics & Gynecology of the British Commonwealth.* Vol. 77, 1970, pp. 333-6.
19. *Amicus Curiae Brief of Some 220 Physicians, Professors and Fellows of the American College of Obstetricians and Gynecologists Before the U.S. Supreme Court in Texas and Georgia Cases.* Oct. term, 1971.
20. Rafael Sevilla, "Oral Feeding of Human Fetus: A Possibility." *JAMA.* May 4, 1970, pp. 713-17.
21. Interview between Mike Levy and Dr. Ballard, *Triumph.* March, 1972. pp. 20-23, 44.
22. Valerie Vance Dillon, "Application for Life." *Sign.* Oct. 1968, p. 12.
23. Dr. H.M.I. Liley, *Modern Motherhood,* Revised Edition. Random House. 1969, p. 50.
24. E. Diamond, *op. cit.* p. 175.
25. Gino Papola, MD, "Abortion Today: A Doctor looks at a modern problem." *L'Osservatore Romano,* March 23, '72, p. 10.
26. H.M.I. Liley, *op. cit.* p. 207.
27. E. Horger & D. Hutchinson M.D., "Diagnostic Use of Amniotic Fluid." *J. of Pediatrics* Vol. 74, No. 3, Sept. 1969, pp. 503-508. W. Floyd, M.D., P. Goodman, & P. Wilson, "CT: Amniotic Fluid Filtration and Cytology." Obstetrics & Gynecology. Vol. 34, No. 4, Oct. 1969. Szijarto, "Modern Diagnostic Criteria of Fetal Suffering." *Fracestoro,* Vol. 61, Nov. - Dec. 1968. Parmley et al., "Fetal Maturity and Amniotic Fluid Analysis." *Am. J. Obstet. & Gynec.*

Vol. 105, No. 3, pp. 354-362.

28. Ashley Montagu, *Life before Birth.* New American Library, 1964, Ch. X.
29. Raleigh Fitkin-Paul Morgan Memorial Hospital v. Anderson, 42 N.J. 421, 201 A. 2d 537, cert denied, 377 U.S. 985 (1964).
30. Peter Berman et al., "A Method for the Prenatal Diagnosis of Congenital Hyperuricemia." *J. of Pediatrics.* Vol. 75, No. 3, Sept. '69. N. O'Doherty, "THe Prenatal Treatment of Adrenal Insufficiency." *The Lancet,* No. 29, '69, 2:1194-95. A. Hodari & T. Lorna, "Experimental Surgical Procedures Upon the Fetus in Obstetric Research." *Obstet. & Gynec.* Vol. 34, No. 2, Aug..69, pp. 204-11.
31. Dillon, *op. cit.* p. 10.
32. Montagu, *op. cit.* pp. 187-8.
33. *Ibid.* p. 178.
34. M. Marcel & J. Exchaquet, "L'Electrocardiogramme du Foetus Human Avec un Cas de Double Rythme Auriculaire Verifiem," *Arch. Mal. Couer.* Paris 31: 504, 1938.
35. Flanagan, *op. cit.* p. 51.
36. Leslie Arey, *Developmental Anatomy,* 6th edition. Saunders Co. 1954, Chs. II, VI.
37. Marcel et al. *op. cit.*
38. Gesell, *op. cit.*
39. Straus et al., *op. cit.*
40. A. Hellegers, "Fetal Development." *Theological Studies.* 3, 7, 1970, p. 26.
41. H.M.I. Liley, *op. cit.* B. Patten, *op. cit.*
42. Liley, op. cit. p, 50. Hooker, *op. cit.* p. 75.
43. Paul Marx, Ph.D., *The Death Peddlers.* St. John's U. Press. 1971, p. 24.
44. Montagu, *op. cit.* p. 186.
45. *Ibid.* "Tobacco Smoke and Other Poisons." p. 99.
46. *Ibid.* p. 97.
47. Cf. Willke, *op. cit.* p. 72. Cf. also A.J. Schaeffer, *Diseases of the Newborn.* Saunders, 1966. ". . .premature birth is the leading cause of infant death, and one of the leading causes of mental and motor retardation."
48. Quoted by Rabbi Karasich in Papola *op. cit.* p. 10 under "Jewish Comments". This remark has been traditionally interpreted as constituting a commandment against killing the unborn child.
49. Dr. Ian Donald, *The Scotsman.* March 9, 1970.
50. "The Abortion Act (1967), "British Medical Journal, 30 May, 1970, p. 533.
51. A.B. Rosenfield et al., "Recent Trends in Infant and Maternal Health in Minnesota," *Minn. Med.* 53:807-16, 1970.
52. Thomas Hilgers, M.D. & Robert Shearin, M.D., "Medical Complications of Induced Abortion." *Induced Abortion: A Documented Report.* Jan. 1971, p. 24.
53. Drs. Gardiner, Pisani & Mattingly, *College Statement and Minority Report on Therapeutic Abortion,* issued by the Am. College of Obstetrics and Gynecology, Chicago, May 1, 1969.
54. J.A. Stallworthy, A.S. Moolgaoker, J.J. Walsh, "Legal Abortion: A Critical Assessment of its Risks," *The Lancet.* Dec. 4, 1971, pp. 1245-49.

55. *Ibid.* p. 1248.
56. S.V. Sood, *Br. Med. J.* 1971, iv, 270.
57. W. Droegemuller et al., "The First Year of Experience in Colorado with the New Abortion Law." *Am. J. Obstet. & Gynec.* 103:694-698, March '69.
58. A.M. Lekhter, "Experience in the Study of the Sequelae to Abortions." Sovet. *Zdravookhr.* 25:27, 1966.
59. L.O. Courtney, *Proc. Roy. Soc. Med.* 62:834, 1969.
60. L.P. Bengtsson et al. "Legal Abortion Induced by Intrauterine injections." (parts I & II) *Lakartidninger,* 64:5037, & 64:5046, 1967.
61. Dr. Paul Popenoe, "Abortion in Japan." *Catholic Digest* (Condensed from *Family Life*) Sept. 1971, p. 28.
62. *Ibid.*
63. M. Ekblad, "Induced Abortion on Psychiatric Grounds, A Follow-Up Study of 479 Women." *Acta. Psychiat. Neurol. Scand. Suppl. 99:238, 1955.*
64. *E. Midak, "Early and Late Sequelae of Abortion." Pol. Tyg. Lek.* 21:1063, 1966.
65. J. Cepelak et al. "Influence of Interruption of Pregnancy on the Sexual Life of the Woman." *Cesk Gynaek.* 25:609, 1960.
66. Quoted by Dr. Paul Marx, O.S.B., "What Sisters Should Know About Abortion." *Sisters Today.* 1972, p. 527.
67. Helene Deutsch, *The Psychology of Women;* A Psychoanalytic Interpretation. Grune & Stratton, 1945. Karl Stern, *The Flight from Woman.* Farrar, Straus & Giroux, 1965, pp. 21-23.
68. R. Le Roux (moderator), "Abortion". *Am.J. Nursing.* 70:1919-1925, '70.
69. Stern, *op. cit.* pp. 22-23.
70. "Spontaneous Induced Abortion," report of a World Health Organization scientific group. *World Health Organization Technical Report Series,* No. 461, p. 41.
71. A. Klinger, "Demographic Consequences of the Legalization of Induced Abortion in Eastern Europe." *Int. J. Gynec. & Obst.* 8:680-691, Sept. 1970, p. 691.
72. *World Health Statistics Report,* Vol. 23, No. 7 pp. 546-549.
73. M. Kuck, "Abortion in Czechoslovakia." *Pro. Roy. Soc. Med.* 62:831-832, 1969.
74. World Health Statistics Report, *op. cit.*
75. Dr. P. Marx, *op. cit.*
76. A. Klinger, *op. cit.*
77. Kotasek, "Artificial Termination of Pregnancy in Czechoslovakia." *Internation Journal of Gynecology and Obstetrics.* Vol 9. Number 3, 1971.
78. M. and A. Wynn, "Some consequences of Induced Abortion to Children born Subsequently." *Foundation for Education and Research in Child-bearing.* London, 1972, p. 12.
79. *Ecclesiastes* 5:14.

THE RIGHT
TO BE
BORN

You are a child of the universe.
No less than the trees and the stars
You have a right to be here.
And whether or not
It is clear to you,
No doubt the universe is unfolding
As it should.

These lines are part of a poem written in 1927 by Max Ehrmann. More recently, in 1972, they appeared as the refrain of the successful popular song entitled *The Desiderata*. No doubt *Desiderata* owes much of its popularity to its gentle poetry and its philosophical calm. But it also contains a truth which often goes unnoticed in the modern age, a truth which is the foundation for anyone's "right to be here".

Some feminists contend that the right to be born is derived exclusively from the mother. Their critics reply that since two people are necessary for intercourse and conception, the right to be born is conferred by both mother and father. Social humanists hold that since society is involved, the right to be born is granted by parents acting in conjunction with social approval. Then there is the view that the right to be born is bestowed by a force which transcends parents and society. This force is aptly symbolized in the first line of *The Desiderata*, "You are a child of the universe." The truth of the matter, and it is a disagreeable one to many, is that human beings are conceived and brought to birth not because of the power of parents or the approval of the public but because of a personal love which cooperates with the power of the universe.

In temporal terms the procreative roles of the parents are momentary in comparison to the eons of evolutionary time used by the universe to tend the slow preparation and intricate development of the egg and sperm. In terms of substance, the parents contribute but one cell apiece, while nature directs the development of all the subsequent trillions. In terms of control, the mating couple merely co-operate, submissively, with a galaxy of forces that surpass their comprehension. In terms of selection, the parents are helpless to determine which sperm and egg will fuse to form the new human being. They do not dominate, develop, and determine their offspring. Rather, they themselves are dwarfed by their unborn and all the cosmic forces which attend his formation. But there is one power parents possess which neither the child nor the universe can contravene. This is the power to negate. Man is free to set his will against the course of the universe and say, "No!" James Oppenheim is right when he states, "Man's the bad seed of the universe."

The "trees and the stars" assert their "right to be here" by virtue of their might. The tree secures itself in the earth with penetrating and tenacious roots. The stars defy dismissal from the universe with their magnitude and incandescence. But the human foetus, not possessing asserting might, clings precariously to his long awaited, slow-brought existence by the tenuous cord of his parents' will.

Here the cosmic paradox is complete. Lifeless matter and unorganized energy from obscure reaches of the universe have collaborated in the most unimaginably complex ways through endless epochs to deliver man to the very threshhold of birth — only to have his advent annulled because the last ingredient in his eternal prescription could not be filled. That last ingredient, seemingly the easiest, was not entrusted to the powerful universe, but to man, who, being free, can choose to negate even the being upon whose soul Time has placed a cosmic seal. Thus, man's free denial, his act of not loving, can bring to nought a lineage which began with the very dawn of creation.

The plan of the universe is not complete until it is accepted through the generosity of human love. The human foetus who awaits his birth or extinction, through affirming love or negating power, had his right to be born purchased for him at a cosmic price that extends over eternity.

Man's basic strength is his power of love. Inversely, his radical weakness is his love of power. The power of love, through affirmation, accepts the rightful course of the universe; the love of power, through negation, seeks to destroy it. The French existentialist Gabriel Marcel has remarked that all temptation may be a temptation towards power — the immoral power to control another.

Love and power are extreme polarities in man's psychological, moral, and religious nature. They are necessarily incompatible. Love for another requires renunciation of power over him; power over another requires renunciation of love. "Where love rules," wrote Carl Jung, "there is no will to power;

and where power predominates, there love is lacking. The one is the shadow of the other."

When man turns his power against other men, he regresses, reversing the course of the universe. This is what happens in abortion. Physical power is exerted over another for the purpose of "progress"; but true progress can take place only through love.

Man's faith in love and his preference for power are sharply contrasted in the abortion debate. The foetus is the most powerless of human beings and therefore the one most in need of human love. At the same time, because he is relatively undeveloped and hidden from view, he is difficult to love and easy to overpower. To condone the willful killing of an unborn human being is to accept as dogma the superiority of power over love. But if man loves, his love is the renunciation of the will to power and the affirmation of eternity.

The noted psychiatrist Karl Stern has drawn an interesting parallel between power and addiction:

> In all cases of addiction there exists an initial sense of *increased freedom,* while in reality the subject becomes increasingly *fettered by necessity.* In the end all freedom is gone, and the subject is encased in a system of forces which are as compelling as the laws which govern inert matter. The drug addict as well as the power addict makes an initial choice to obtain some thing, and before he realizes it that thing has obtained him.

The cry for more permissive abortion legislation is consistent with the profile of the power addict. These demands are always expressed in terms of *more:* more freedom, more control, more money, more opportunities, more power. It is as if the power addict cannot act until all life's obstacles have been cleared from his path. But the one who loves is never at a loss to express his love and to live with peace and contentment under the most adverse and humble conditions.

Some idealistic philosophers and some Christian clergymen have been supporting an unrealistic and unchristian phenomenon which has been gaining popularity. This phenomenon involves a dislocation in time and space — a spiritual alienation from the present moment and the nearby person.

The realistic philosopher affirms the reality of the present. The future is not. He also affirms the absolute value of all human beings, nearby or far away, impoverished or affluent, diseased or healthy, retarded or intelligent. He knows that men possess an intrinsic value which, when recognized, makes them lovable. Therefore, according to the philosopher of realism, men love those they know, those nearby, those they can touch.

Similarly, the Christian works out his salvation in a series of present moments. He is told by Christ that, "The evil of the day is sufficient thereof." He is counselled to love his neighbor as himself. Thus, the Christian as well as the realistic philosopher is concerned with immediacy in time and space: caring for one's neighbor today.

Unrealistic, unchristian thinkers find their neighbor unlovable and their present situation unlivable. Distressed by and impatient with what immediately surrounds them, they look to future generations, dreaming of a better life created out of their own wisdom and power. They exchange the dying friend for a painless ideal and call it *euthanasia*. They replace the growing foetus with a future plan and call it *therapeutic abortion*. They forsake tradition to fight a war they cannot understand and call it *social consciousness*. They are like Don Quixote, filled with energy but deluded by romantic visions into attacking windmills.

Nicolas Berdyaev poses the following question in his brilliant work on Dostoevsky:

> Has a very unusual man, who is called to the service of his fellows, the right to kill a specimen of the lowest sort of human creature, who is only a source of evil to others . . . with the sole object of contributing to the future good of mankind?

The question is profound, epic, eternal. But for the Christian, it is not even problematic. "Whatsoever you do to the least of My Brethren, that you do unto Me." Nor is it problematic for Dostoevsky, who, as artist, psychologist, philosopher, and man, puts forward his position with unsurpassed skill. Berdyaev continues:

> Ivan in *The Brothers Karamazov*, presents this question to his brother Alyosha: Suppose that you are building up a fabric of human destiny with the object of making people happy at last and giving them peace and rest, but that in order to do so it is necessary and unavoidable to torture a single tiny baby . . . and to found your building on its tears — would you agree to undertake the building on that condition?

But who is Ivan Karamazov? Is he a genuine humanitarian? Or is he the devil? Dostoevski gives his answer dramatic force by having Satan speak to Ivan in a dream:

> You are an incarnation of myself but of only one side of me — of my thoughts and feelings, and only the nastiest and stupidest of them. . . . You are myself, myself — but with a different face. . . . You are not someone else; You and I, and nothing more. You are nothing — only my own fancy.

Man builds a better world only through a patient love of the universe and of the God who directs its power. Derivatively, ." There is no other way. If man will not love, he is nothing — nothing but the devil's fancy.

A child has a right to be born because he is a child of the universe and the God who directs its power. Derivatively, he has a right to be born for other reasons: 1) because of his intrinsic excellence as a human form; 2) because of the goodness and lovableness which he is by nature; 3) because he is called into being by his parents, and consistency and responsibility require that birth follow conception; 4) because his destiny is to be happy; 5) because he is innocent; 6) because parents and society have a duty to promote all that is human.

To refuse a child his rightful birth is to refuse him everything he is entitled to receive. It is to deny him his right to inherit the earth. The abortionists want the earth for themselves and are loathe to share it with more people than they deem absolutely necessary.

While Hannah Arendt prepared her book *Eichmann in Jerusalem,* she was struck by the easeful consciences of Eichmann and many of his fellow exterminators. For them evil had become a banality that could no longer activate their moral conscience. Miss Arendt closed the epilogue with what she believed to be the most judicious pronouncement that could be passed on Adolf Eichmann:

> And just as you supported and carried out a policy of not wanting to share the earth with the Jewish people and the people of a number of other nations — as though you and your superiors had any right to determine who should and who should not inhabit the world — we find that no one, that is, no member of the human race, can be expected to want to share the earth with you. This is the reason, and the only reason, you must hang.

—9—

THE FOETUS: HIS HUMANITY AND HIS RIGHTS

We know what something is when we know its causes. From Aristotle to the present, this stricture has remained universally respectable. While there have been various opinions expressed throughout history concerning which of Aristotle's four causes should be investigated in any given discipline and how these privileged causes should be approached, they have, nonetheless, enjoyed a time honored usage, providing invaluable objective correlatives for a major part of Western philosophical and scientific thought.

We ask the question, "what is that something which exists within a human mother and develops over a nine month period until its time of birth?" There is speculation that this something is "human". But the word "human" seems at once both highly appropriate and highly inappropriate. Further reflection reveals that the word "human" is not always used univocally in describing the human foetus and the human adult; nor is the word "human" used univocally in describing a human achievement and human hair. However, the ambiguity of the word "human" is resolved when each of its four different senses is related to each of the four traditional Aristotelian causes. In this way, the discussion of how the word "human" is applied to the foetus gains the objective advantages that a correlation with Aristotle's four causes naturally provides.

The four causes represent a hierarchic order, the higher causes subsuming the lower causes. Thus, the final cause, which sets into motion the other three causes and is said to be the cause of causes, subsumes the formal, material, and efficient causes; the formal cause, for which the material cause exists, subsumes the material and efficient causes; the material cause, which requires an impetus from its immediately prior efficient cause in order for it to come into being, subsumes the efficient cause.

SUMMARY TABLE:

Cause(s)	Uses of the word "Human"	Verb specifying the act which relates the cause(s) to its (their) "human" effects	Mode of application to the foetus
Efficient	human achievement	makes	not a real application
Efficient, Material	human part	produces	under-application
Efficient, Material, Formal	human form	procreates	proper application (although imperfect)
Efficient, Material, Formal, Final	human being	perfects	over-application (over-application to a mature adult, although to a considerably lesser degree)

Four uses of the word "human", and their mode of application to the foetus are set forth below in correlation with each of the four causes taken in ascending hierarchic order.

As Efficient Cause:

The efficient cause is extrinsic to its effect. Also, as immediately prior to its effect, it is not, as such, directly involved in its effect's final ordination or perfection. For these two reasons, the efficient cause tells us less about its effect than do any of the other causes.

We speak of great art works or great engineering feats as "remarkable *human* achievements". In this way, we distinguish them from natural wonders and attribute to them human efficient causality. Human art is "human" primarily because it is *made* by humans. However, insofar as humans merely make things, nothing which is materially human inheres in what is made. This use of the word "human", therefore, has no substantial or real application to the foetus; it is used only to describe an artifact such as a model of a human foetus which is employed for instructional purposes.

As Efficient and Material Causes:

The material cause tells us about the fundamental intrinsic makeup of a thing. It does not specify the form or the nature of a being, but describes its composing parts.

We speak of *human* hair, *human* skin, or *human* protoplasm. In this sense, the word "human" denotes not only something which is efficiently caused by a human, but something which contains human matter. Human hair, as well as any other human part, contains human substance.

Properly speaking, the human organism *produces* human parts, as the liver produces bile or the salivary glands produce saliva. Here the word "human" under-applies to the foetus because the foetus is not produced by one human organism, nor is it a material part of a human organism.

As Efficient, Material, and Formal Causes:

The formal cause tells us about the specific organization of a being, its nature or formal constitution. It tells us more than does the material cause by specifying how a being's totality is served by the functioning of all its material parts.

We speak of a *human* form to denote an empirically identifiable human entity, or human organism. Properly speaking, *human* forms or *human* organisms are *procreated* by human parents. The word procreate implies that the offspring is more than a material part produced by another; the offspring enjoys a human, organismic form of its own. Since the foetus is a human form, or a human organism, the word "human" in its formal sense properly applies.

However, from the foetus's earliest moment of actuality, development, or movement, he is under the influence of that finality toward which his organismic vitality tends him. Hence, he participates, to a degree, in a final human form that perfects and completes his present organismic human form. The word "human" in its formal sense, therefore, applies properly but imperfectly to him.

As Efficient, Material, Formal, and Final Causes:

The final cause adds the note of perfection, of completing all that the subject is supposed to complete. It adds to a form which is empirically identifiable as human a perfection which is normatively identifiable as human.

We speak of a *human* being to denote one who has everything he should have in order to be fully human, the adult, the mature person. However, to be absolutely precise, there are no perfected human beings and here the word "human" refers to human forms who are well on their way toward realizing a host of human perfections.

Properly speaking, one *perfects* himself in becoming more truly a human being. In this sense, the word "human" over-applies to the foetus. However, it should be added that it also somewhat over-applies to even saints. Nonetheless, one is more human the more he approximates his final cause, the more he identifies with what he ought to be.

The Foetus and Human Rights:

There is no intrinsic dynamic tendency that moves from a human achievement (or artifact) to a human part (*The Picture of Dorian Gray,* notwithstanding), or from a human achievement (or artifact) to a human form (Pygmalion, notwithstanding), or from a human part to a human form (the formation of Minerva from Jupiter's forehead, notwithstanding). However, there is an intrinsic dynamic tendency within a living human form (such as the foetus, properly speaking) which moves toward a more perfect form (the human being, properly speaking). The foetus as an active human form tends toward his perfection as a more complete human being; the empirical human who *is* tends, by his own natural weight, to become the normative human who *ought to be.* Because of this natural, active tendency in humans, from form to finality, we say that everyone has a *right* to become what he ought to be. The claim to be more perfect, to become what one ought to become, is recognized in the very fact of that dynamic tendency which expresses itself in the development of the human foetus. The foetus, from its incipience, is involved in his finality; the saint, in the most glorious moments of his humanity, does not realize the absolute fulfillment of his finality. The foetus as well as the saint are both, to borrow Heidegger's expression, "moving into the nearness of distance."

The rights of the foetus, therefore, are his natural claims to preserve and develop the dynamic tendency which is the intrinsic expression of his human form, so that he is able to participate more fully in that finality which is perfective of his being.

Human freedom, then, to quote Heidegger once more, is "the letting be of what is." "Letting be" allows "what ought to be" to emanate; "what is" is the human form that presents the claim to be what it ought to be.

In a just and loving, democratic society, the human right of the foetus to be allowed to become more fully human is recognized and protected. In an authoritarian and power-oriented, totalitarian society, this right is neither recognized nor protected.

The fact that the foetus exists and develops within a human mother who has human rights of her own, complicates the pragmatics of abortion where there is or appears to be a conflict of rights between the mother and her foetus. However, no degree of pragmatic complexity should obscure 1) the real claim the foetus has for the recognition and protection of his human rights and 2) his status as a human form already intimately involved in his finality, at once a human form and a dynamic process of becoming a more perfect human being.

—10—

LIFE OR LIBERTY? SMOKE AND REVOLUTION

"O Liberty, how many crimes are committed in thy name!" Madame Roland said, mounting the scaffold. "Is life so dear and peace so sweet as to be purchased at the price of chains and slavery?" exclaimed Patrick Henry. These two comments, one originating in the aftermath of the French Revolution, the other in the prelude to the American Revolution, could just as well have been uttered by an anti-abortionist and a pro-abortionist, respectively. Of what value is *liberty,* an anti-abortionist might ask, if it leads to the premature death of an innocent human foetus? Of what value is *life,* a pro-abortionist might retort, if it enslaves a mother to an unwanted child?

At this point, the most common form of the abortion debate is stalemated. Which is more important, the *liberty* of the mother or the *life* of the foetus? Which should have priority? Who can decide? The issue appears unresolvable. Perhaps, as some argue, since no universally acceptable solution to this dilemma has come forth, laws restricting abortion should be repealed. Each pregnant woman would then be free to decide the abortion issue for herself. Would that not be the most *reasonable, fair,* and *practical* arrangement?

From another point of view, it would be a most *unreasonable, unfair,* and *impractical* arrangement. The reason that the life vs. liberty argument goes nowhere is that it makes no sense in the first place.

Life, taken by itself, unadorned by liberty, love, justice, hope, or any of the other factors which sustain life, is non-existent. It is a fiction, an empty abstraction, a mere idea. Similarly, liberty, taken by itself, dissociated from life, duty, responsibility, purpose, and all the other factors which secure liberty, is also non-existent. It is a false reality, a formless vapor, a mere velleity. Nowhere does life or liberty exist as a pure isolated, independent entity. That is why the life vs. liberty debate is unproductive. Two unreal parents cannot produce a real child. The solution to the dilemma is in avoiding it initially.

Life and liberty confer value upon one another. Liberty crowns life, and life expands liberty. Realistically, they are inseparable; they can be taken apart only mentally. Likewise, any argument which pits environment against heredity, man against woman, offense against defense, is unresolvable because none of those factors exists independently of the other.

The very fact that there are sides in the abortion issue implies a fundamental misunderstanding. Since life and liberty go together, presumably everyone should be on the side of life and liberty. There simply isn't any other side. Maybe it's partly due to man's sporting sense or his competitive instinct that he prefers to choose sides. But in moral matters there is only one side — the human side, the side of life and liberty taken together.

It is difficult for a person to choose always on the side of life and liberty. Man is a socially interdependent being, incapable of attaining moral or human self-sufficiency by himself. No man is an island. Man needs others in order to overcome his incompleteness. Therein is the great value of society. Where one person is weak, another is strong. Where one woman cannot rear her child, another wants to adopt one. In a society where moral complementarity were the rule, a life vs. liberty debate would be unnecessary. An unwanted pregnancy problem would be resolved in terms of, *How can life-and-liberty best be served for all concerned?*

Pro-abortionists argue that no law should require a pregnant woman to carry an unwanted foetus to term. But this argument presupposes that such a law acts negatively. On the contrary, laws that restrict abortion encourage society to offer the pregnant woman all its positive resources. Secondly, the argument presupposes the reasonableness of solving, in an asocial manner, a problem which has deep social implications.

A morally complementary society consolidates its strength to lessen the difficulties and distresses of pregnancy. When carrying a pregnancy to term means losing employment or interrupting education, such a society can provide appropriate compensations. Where physical, emotional, or financial needs are present, it can rally to the aid of the pregnant woman in innumerable positive and beneficial ways.

Abortion is a very lonely experience. It epitomizes the dislocation of the person from society, society's failure to offer moral aid at a time of moral crisis, societal abandonment when the woman is most in need of social integration.

The woman who has an abortion spares herself the temporary inconvenience of a full-term pregnancy. But the liberty she gains does not counterbalance the forfeiture of her societal benefits, society's humanizing values, her aborted child's life and liberty, and the love and joy of parenthood.

The maximum realization of life-and-liberty values appears comfortably on the side of birth, not abortion.

The *reasonable, fair,* and *practical* approach, therefore, would be not to change abortion laws in the direction of moral abandonment but to reform society in the direction of moral complementarity. Which is the more human society: One where the individual is dislocated from society and given the unrealistic task of being morally autonomous, or one where there is cooperative moral solidarity?

This is not an unrealistic plea for a moral utopia. It is simply a logical and positive development of those basic principles which any humanistic society must adopt if it is to survive and prosper. No one should feel isolated from the moral assistance of society.

The way the abortion debate is resolved will go a long way toward determining the kind of society in which people believe. If they believe in a society which protects and fosters life and liberty, they will see a striking incompatibility between that society and the one which chooses permissive abortion.

"ALL'S RIGHT WITH THE WORLD!"

> When to infinity the one thing
> Self-repeating ever flows,
> The thousandfold divided arches
> Firmly fitting each in each,
> Then streams life-joy from every object,
> The smallest and the greatest star,
> And every strife, and every conflict
> Find eternal peace in God.

> —Goethe, "Zahme Xenien"

In viewing Giorgio de Chirico's surrealistic painting "Furniture in the Countryside", one is immediately struck by its central incongruity. What is furniture doing in the countryside? The sharp clash of an indoor suite against an outdoor background creates a sense of discordant relationship — what communication specialist Marshall McLuhan might term "abrasive interface". Philosophically, it calls to mind a basic principle of phenomenology: that it is *relationship* rather than *being* that initially provokes attention.

Beings never appear in isolation, but always within a network of inter-relationships with other beings. Consequently, beings are perceived and evaluated in a context, not so much by what they are but by how they resonate (with good or bad vibrations) with neighboring objects. A candle is holy on an altar, romantic on a piano, eerie in a jack-o-lantern, and elegant on a table. Toys clutter a dining table but complement a Christmas tree. A Stetson might be smart atop one's head, but on the ice of a hockey rink it becomes debris. William Blake reflected this common form of perception when he wrote:

> A Robin Redbreast in a Cage
> Puts all heaven in a rage.

According to McLuhan, the meaning of relationship arises in the resonating interval which separates the boundaries of adjacent entities. In his book *Take Today: Executive as Dropout,* he discusses this resonating interval as the interplay of *figure* and *ground.*

These terms (used widely by psychologists and psychotherapists) can be discriminated quite readily. A word, for example, is a *figure* in a sentence which is its *ground.* The sentence is *a figure* within a certain cultural sphere which is its *ground.* Thus, a word can be fully understood only in the context of a definite sentence; a sentence can be fully understood only in the context of a certain cultural sphere. It may be appropriate for scientists to isolate *figure* and *ground,* to conceptualize it as a singular entity for the purposes of classification, but in ordinary perception *figure* and *ground* are regarded as inseparable.

The *figure-ground* distinction may be helpful toward understanding an apparently anomalous position espoused by certain pro-abortionists. Although willing to accord the foetus his humanity, these pro-abortionists are unwilling to extend to him his right to live whenever he is unwanted. In their minds, being unwanted, an evaluation of *relationship,* takes precedence over being human, an assessment of *being.* They view abortion, therefore, not so much as an attack against a human being as a decision against an unwanted relationship.

This particular pro-abortion attitude may be viewed in the light of *figure-ground* relationships. The foetus who emerges from a *ground* of love (positive resonance or rightfulness) is deliverable. The foetus who emerges from a *ground* of contraceptive sex, lust, or forcible rape (negative resonance or "abrasive interface"), in the view of pro-abortionists, is abortable. In neither case is the foetus appraised in isolation. In the former instance the foetus is the incarnation of love, where *ground* becomes *figure* in a dynamically creative process. In the latter instance the *figure* which results from the resonating interval is rejected, as if the full reality of the resonating interval had not been affirmed in the first place. In other words, if meaning does indeed arise in the resonant interval between two things, and if a human foetus can result from sexual union, then accepting the unborn is accepting also the full natural meaning of sexual intercourse; rejecting the unborn is rejecting also the full natural meaning of sexual intercourse.

Pro-abortionists who are not especially concerned about the fact that the foetus is human establish their relational attitude toward the foetus apart from any consideration of the natural continuity that exists between sexual union and the generation of the foetus or the moral continuity that exists between the foetus's essential call to be cared for which is inscribed within his being and the human response which answers that call for care. They are concerned solely with what they regard to be the freely determined attitudes of 'wanted' and 'unwanted'. The force of an unwanted relationship can be so strong as to obscure completely the rightful relationship between the foetus and the sexual union which called him into existence as well as his intrinsic human value. On the strength of a negative relationship (unwantedness) these abortionists are willing to dissociate procreation from sex, devalue the human nature of the foetus, and ignore his intrinsic call to be cared for. In this way, they sever *figure* (the foetus) from *ground* (sex) and rightful relationship (caring) from being (the foetus's essential call to be cared for), contending that the primarily relevant guidelines according to which the abortion question should be resolved are subjective and arbitrary, and not natural and moral.

Pro-life advocates maintain that to be a human being is to present an intrinsic claim to be cared for, that rightful relationship is not equivocally related to being but univocally determined by it. The pro-abortionists argue that being human (in the case of the foetus) is equivocally or discontinuously related to relationship to that being.

The natural continuity of sexual union and procreation together with the moral continuity of being and rightful relationship to that being, form a fundamental, dynamic, and positively resonating pattern which is open to being united communally with other patterns of similar form and movement. The being of sexual union in continuity with its rightful relationship to conception, the foetus in continuity with his rightful relationship with those who care for him, form but a part of a series of *figure-ground, being-relationship* patterns that ultimately delineate the Divine Plan.

The ultimate *ground* of man as creature is God the Creator. Between God and uncreated man the silent space of the void was filled with an energy called Love and man was created. In the words of the poet, theologian, and philosopher Teilhard de Chardin, "love as energy" is "affinity of being with being". Thus, love as relationship is a harmony between beings, where relationship and being become indistinguishably one. When the interval between Being and being is charged with Love, creation takes place. Man, in turn, through loving sexual union, extends Love through procreation, and returns to God by keeping His Law. God's Love proves its affinity with prospective man by the fact of creation; parents' love proves its affinity with their prospective offspring by the fact of conception; man's love proves its affinity with God by his atonement (at-one-ment) with God. The movement from *ground* to created *figure* to procreated *figure* ultimately finds its completion in a return to God. Love is the creative resonance which allows this advance and return. In *The Phenomenon of Man,* Chardin hears the cosmic music of creative Love by which all things move toward the

Omega and speaks of "Resonance to the All — the keynote of pure poetry and pure religion."

Abortion, in separating *ground* from *figure,* relationship from being, is a decision that favors essential human disharmony. It is also a choice for closure in the universe; an opting for the energy of love to abate, to be rendered effete. Ultimately it is a falling out of step with the cadence of theocentric evolution. Loving, caring procreation, as a continuation of creation, preserves relationship with God and extends the resonance of love in the form of a communal dynamism whose ultimate end is re-union with the Creator. Abortion, in refusing to allow *figure* to emerge from *ground,* characterizes that *ground* as loveless, rejects the full reality implied by the resonant interval of sexual union, and expresses a preference for stagnation and self-contained entities above a dynamic and communal return to God. Consequently, abortion, in separating relationship from its root in being, breaks the cycle of Love that began within God and was destined to return to Him in man, who, by ever keeping the relationship of his love close to the being of his humanity, would have always remained a faithful vessel for transmitting God's eternal Word.

Positively resonating intervals, where relationship and being vibrate in unison, are in harmony with God's plan and the movement of Love through the universe. Regarding the relationship of parent to foetus as arbitrary or elective represents a disconnection from the flow of that Love. Negatively resonating intervals, where relationship is uprooted from its home in being, are sterile, inverted, not "in-place" (to use Milton Meyerhoff's expression), or "out of joint" (to quote Macbeth). Examples of negatively resonating intervals are found in the opening lines of G.K. Chesterton's *The Donkey:*

> When fishes flew and forests walked
> And figs grew upon thorn,
> Some moment when the moon was blood
> Then surely was I born.

The essential structure (being) of fishes is out of harmony with the act of flying. So too, the being of forests is not consonant with ambulation. Tender figs, as figures, could not be grounded in thorns, no more than animate blood could be inanimate moon. Nothing is right in such a world, because act never flows from form, relationship never proceeds from being. There can be no faith in such a world, because there is no continuity, no cycle, no Divine return.

Positively resonating intervals preserve continuity, direction, love, energy, harmony, and Godliness. They represent belonging, caring, being "in-place". "We are *in place*", writes Meyerhoff, "in the world through having our lives ordered by inclusive caring." Heidegger, the philosopher of care, sees man as "Da-sein" — "being-there-in-place-in-the-world". The positive resonance resulting from man's authentic dwelling resounds throughout the world. In poetic terms, Robert Browning captures the serenity and beauty of the positive resonance that results from things' being in their proper place, where *figure-ground* relationships are harmonious and open to transcendence:

> The year's at the spring
> And the day's at the morn;
> Morning's at seven;
> The hillside's dew-pearled;
> The lark's on the wing;
> The snail's on the thorn:
> God's in his heaven —
> All's right with the world!

—12—
THE POLES OF THE PARADOX: SPEAKERS FOR STEREOPHONIC THOUGHT

> It was the best of times, it was the worst of times, it was the age of wisdom, it was the age of foolishness, it was the epoch of belief, it was the epoch of incredulity, . . .

This familiar opening passage from Charles Dicken's *A Tale of Two Cities* is a succession of striking paradoxes which unite seemingly incompatible states. The co-existence of these opposing actualities, perhaps a little startling to Dickens's readers, nonetheless provides an appropriate vehicle for ushering in his most dramatic novel. Drama, as well as thought itself, cannot exist apart from the tension created by opposition. For drama is to a novel as the paradox is to thought: each stimulating awareness by what it reveals, each sustaining interest by what it withholds.

The Western writer commonly presents the paradoxical situation as anomalous, unusual or enigmatic. For the most part his works abound in clear logic and simple concepts. Paradox is heterodox. To the Eastern writer, on the other hand, the paradox describes an elementary condition, a recognized verity. Paradox is orthodox. In Chinese, for example, the ideogram for the word crisis consists of two characters, of which one stands for opportunity, the other for danger. Zen-Buddhists refer to a fundamental tenet of Eastern thinking when they write: "The way is no way". In both word and philosophy, the Easterner is very much at home with the paradox, while the Westerner puzzles over its dual implications.

Bertrand Russell, true to the Western analytic spirit, in his *Mathematica Principia,* published in 1913, sought to reduce all of mathematics to logic. He believed that since the expression "mathematical paradox" was simply a cover for ignorance of logic, all mathematical paradoxes could be conquered by dividing them into separate logical identities or tautologies. He argued that all mathematical statements could be expressed as subject-predicate identities. For example, "one plus one is two" is a logical identity because each side of the equation expresses the same thing. In other words, "two" is just a shorthand way of writing "one plus one". Extending this concept of analytic logic beyond mathematics, Russell devised a philosophy of *logical atomism,* according to which the world is composed of facts absolutely independent of each other. For Russell, logic dissolved the mystery of the paradox by dividing it into component tautologies, thus reducing the world to a set of manageable atomic facts which provided a rational basis for "human progress".

But the real paradox, having no atomic parts, is not decomposable. Its polarity represents so fundamental an order of relationship that, like the process of living and dying, it cannot be segregated into discrete elements. Furthermore, having a predicate always surprisingly different from its subject, it contradicts the basic assumption of analytic logic. Contrary to Russell's basis for "human progress", the paradox suggests that analysis is paralysis.

Hegel's dictum "Being is Nothing" represents a break in the line of traditional Western thought; the logic of "both/and" in favor of the logic of "either/or". "Nothing" is the unexpected predicate of "Being". It is both "Being" as well as "not-Being". In the tautology, "A" is either "B" or "not-B"; in the paradox, "A" is both "B" and "not-B". For Hegel, the opposition between Being and Nothing was dynamic, giving rise to the reciprocal passage of Being into Nothing, and Nothing into Being which is resolved in the paradox of Becoming. He termed traditional logical tautologies "boring pleonasms" which reflected nothing of reality.

Tautologies are closed, predictable, one-dimensional, and monaural; paradoxes are open, unpredictable, multi-dimensional, and stereophonic. What the tautology gains in clarity it loses in depth; what it gains in simplicity it loses in truth.

Other philosophers, atypical to the Western tradition, have expressed the core of their philosophy in the form of a paradox. Dionysius, an ancient Greek thinker, centered his natural philosophy of the Divinity on the notion that God is known as unknown. Aquinas taught that "what is first in intention is last in execution"; that the final cause is logically contemporaneous with the efficient cause. Martin Buber envisioned man's primary reality in the form of "I-Thou". Heidegger saw man's authentic dwelling on earth as taking place within the oscillating duality between thinking and building *(bauen).* T. S. Eliot uses the following statement from Heraclitus for the epigraph of perhaps his most philosophical poem. "Burnt Norton": "The way upward and downward are one and the same".

The paradox recognizes the dynamic inter-relationships between co-existing opposites and presents reality in its richness and openness. Single-valued tautologies are fine for mathematical precision, but they fail to describe the real situation. In trying to perceive the reality of one-dimensional entities, one finds himself straining to hear the sound of one hand clapping or searching the sky for footprints left by birds. For such reasons Wyndham Lewis exclaimed, "There is nothing so impressive as the number TWO." The poles of the paradox are the flint and friction that spark action. The paradox is a form of truth that reflects reality's fullness. Carl Jung writes:

> Oddly enough, the paradox is one of our most valued spiritual possessions, while uniformity of meaning is a sign of weakness. Hence a religion becomes inwardly impoverished when it loses or reduces its paradoxes; but their multiplication enriches, because only the paradox comes anywhere near to comprehending the fullness of life.

Tertullian's test of theological truth, *"Certum est, quia impossibile est"* (It is certain, because it is impossible), is designed to keep reality larger than a formulated phrase. E. E. Cumming's test of poetic truth, "the truest things are true because they can't be true", acknowledges the reality of the incomprehensible. The paradox preserves the metaphysical aspect of things and resists their being reduced to classified items. Tautologies make things easier to assimilate mentally, but they leave out their mystery and consequently their truth. "With everyone engaged everywhere in making things easier", wrote Kierkegaard, "someone was needed to make them difficult again."

One-sidedness, half-truths, moral tautologies and over-simplifications can be dangerously misleading. Such is the case with much of the pro-abortion rhetoric. The assertion that the foetus belongs exclusively to the pregnant mother is a one-sided simplification of a complex reality. The poet-philosopher Kahlil Gibran, in characteristic paradoxical style writes:

> Your children are not your children
> They are the sons and daughters of Life's longing for itself.
> They come through you but not from you,
> And though they are with you yet they belong not to you.

Parents are entrusted with children, but do not own them. They influence their children's destinies, but do not determine them. They guard without controlling; protect without smothering. They love without being covetous; encourage without being impatient. There is no single attitude or defined stance which captures the parent-child relationship. The child is neither simply an individual nor simply a product of the mother's body. The woman who says, "I'll never surrender the right to control my own body", is like the caterpillar who says to the butterfly, "You'll never catch me up in one of those danged things."

All authentic human relationships are expressed in the form of "We". Plurality is more elementary than singularity. Emerson warned, "Don't leave the sky out of your landscape". The form of singleness is also the form of loneliness, of aching incompleteness. Nature marries each being with its other. Reasoning in isolation, unmindful of one's connection with the world, results in making creeds without legs for men without hearts.

Human relationships are not autonomously determined, they are heteronomously experienced. The answer to the question "Whose child is this?" is best framed in a paradox. The simplistic answer belies a poverty of experience. Babies are aborted because of an unexperienced or unremembered "We".

III

RESTORING MISSING VALUES

"Let parents, then, bequeath to their children not riches, but the spirit of reverence."

— Plato

THE PRIMACY
OF
CARE

Around Christmas time, after the regular football season has ended, an All-Star game in San Francisco's Kezar Stadium pits the best seniors from the East against the best from the West. This event, the Shrine Game, is played for the benefit of crippled children. Its motto is: "Strong legs run so that weak legs may walk." Before their gridiron contest, the players visit San Francisco's hospital for crippled children to meet the youngsters for whom they will be playing and to present them with gifts. When Cornell's 1971 All-American, record-breaking fullback Ed Marinaro, visited these innocent victims of disease and deformity, he confessed that if there was anything decent he'd ever done in his life, this was it.

The motto of the Shrine Game elicits a human response that is so intimate to man's fundamental nature as to coincide with it. This response is *care*. How easy it is for people to forget its primary and essential value!

The value of strong legs is never better actualized than when they run to help others. Strength is never stronger than when it is offered as a gift. Some people boast of their strength as if it were only a private adornment. But exhibitionism is seldom inspirational. As a matter of fact, it is usually boring. While strength of any kind is good in itself, it does not become a moral good until it is enlisted in the service of care.

At Boys Town, Nebraska, there is a motto similar to that of the Shrine Game: "He ain't heavy, Father . . . he's m' brother." Care lightens physical burdens because, being so fundamental to man, it releases energies which allow him to become more fully alive, capable of more readily surmounting difficulties and enduring hardships. Care also lightens spiritual or mental burdens because it gives purpose and meaning to man's natural abilities. Why is one intelligent? So that he can teach others. Why is one musical? So that he can bring music into the lives of others. In an age when the purpose and meaning of life are so often displaced by existential anxiety, care has enormous therapeutic value.

The essential human value of care, being an item of special interest to artists and philosophers, has been variously represented throughout history. But perhaps the most beautiful portrayal of care is found in an ancient Roman myth, where the essential meaning of care is revealed in an allegory of great simplicity and richness.

One day Care was amusing herself by molding earth into various shapes. She fashioned one shape which especially appealed to her. Wanting this new form to enjoy life, she beseeched Jupiter to grant it a soul. Jupiter obliged Care by breathing life into the earthly form. Care then requested that this new creature be named after her. When Jupiter objected, they asked Saturn, the god of Time, to serve as arbiter. Saturn decreed that when the new creature died, its body must return to Earth, which was its origin; its soul must return to its father, Jupiter, who gave it life. But all the Time it was alive it was to be entrusted to Care.

According to this fable, while man lives on earth his truest name is care. That is to say, man essentially is care. When he ceases to care, he ceases to be man.

It is also true that those who most need care can best elicit it from those who have it to offer. This truth explains why Ed Marinaro feels that crippled children do more for him by presenting their need than do the countless fans and sports writers who praise his football heroics. "Whatsoever you do for the least of my little ones, that you do unto Me," is a statement that brings together the one who most needs care with the One who best gives it.

To be crippled is a great physical misfortune, but the greatest human misfortune is to be uncared for, because the deserted person does not know another person as precisely human. Being uncared for means to lack the primarily and essentially human form of unification with other men. While being uncared for is a human evil, not caring is a moral evil. It is the greatest moral evil, in general, because it is a human stance devoid of human heart. It may be the greatest human evil, in particular, when it deserts the most helpless, most care-needing person of all, the child in the womb.

We express much concern about pollution, population, war, violence, starvation, poverty, inflation, and unemployment. But the greatest evil contemporary man faces is not caring for his fellow man. When Mother Teresa of India arrived in Canada in the Fall of 1971, she offered these words:

> The biggest disease today is not leprosy or tuberculosis, but rather the feeling of being unwanted, uncared for and deserted by everybody.

Some writers argue that *freedom,* not care, is the most basic human value. Accordingly, a woman ought to be given the legal freedom to choose for herself whether or not she will carry her child to term.

The contention that freedom is the original and essential human value is based on the illusion that freedom is a value in itself. However, freedom has value only when it is given away. An analogy may make this point clear.

A person owns a ticket to a Stanley Cup hockey game. The ticket symbolizes his freedom to witness that event. Thinking about the ticket and anticipating the game, he rejoices. But if he wants to retain the ticket, he must forego the hockey game. In order to see the game, he must relinquish his ticket at the door of the arena.

Freedom is valuable only when it is cashed in for what one desires. It is something like trading stamps, of importance only because it can be redeemed for something else. Care, on the other hand, is a vlaue in itself because it coincides with the value that is man.

Thus, freedom is in the service of care, being important only because care is more important. When one refuses to care, his freedom is valueless.

Why, then, is there so much furor over freedom and so little concern over care? One reason may be that caring for others is not marketable. Too many people have been virtually mesmerized by commercial advertising into believing that material possessions, gracious living, and independence from others are much more humanly satisfying than caring for others. Many women believe that finer clothes, a larger house, or a better paying job are more fundamental life concerns than caring for an unborn child.

Another reason may be that freedom itself, because it has no content, appears to the imagination to represent an infinite number of desirable possibilities. Caring for another appears to offer but one grim, undesirable reality. But freedom, as a mere possibility, remains valueless until it is surrendered for the one reality that is cared for. One cared-for reality is more valuable than an infinity of uncared-for possibilities.

A third reason may be that caring implies a fixed responsibility, whereas freedom promises adventure. The lure of the Tropics, the charm of Europe, the mystery of the Orient, possibilities fired by the breath of freedom, are superficially more attractive than remaining dedicated to the dull and determinable care of a child.

Finally, freedom may deceptively promise an exemption from inconvenience and pain. Caring requires that in accepting another's burden, one must share his inconvenience and pain. But to remain suspended in a world of illusory possibilities, protected from the pain and inconvenience of care, is to refuse to live. This kind of freedom is a death wish.

Valuing freedom above care, whatever reason one may give, is a flight from being human. But if one flees his humanity, he leaves behind the part that is more important; like the man who sent his baggage off on vacation while he remained at home.

The abortion debate touches upon an ageless human conflict. Will a pregnant woman hear and respond to the call for care that beats within her, or, because she is ambitious, will she choose to listen elsewhere, across a vast freedom-spanned ocean, for a sound that will find her heart? Will man accept, humbly, the limiting conditions defined by his nature as care, or will he gamble on boundless freedom in the wild hope that it will carry him beyond his weary lot? "I charge thee, fling away ambition: By that sin fell the angels." This timeless admonition, reiterated by Shakespeare, suggests how far one may fall pursuing total freedom.

The growing social tolerance toward not wanting or not caring for the unborn is accompanied with an intolerance toward restrictions on personal freedom. Today, more people believe that permissive laws are a reliable index of social progress. Yet, there is only one thing which man needs — to be related through care to others in his society.

The mother who chooses an abortion not only prevents the emergence of life in another, but suppresses the emergence of human life in herself. If she undergoes an abortion because freedom is more important to her than care, she will find no ultimate justification for that choice. It has been said of Mary that, "In the bankruptcy of reason, she alone was real." In today's society, which so irrationally fears the future, care for the human unborn is both most real and most needed.

—14—

IS MANKIND AN OBJECT OF LOVE?

How easy it is, remarked Dostoevsky, for a person, on the one hand, to approach ecstasy while meditating on the excellence of mankind; and on the other hand, to be driven to distraction by one particular man's unpleasant way of blowing his nose. This paradox illustrates how comfortable man can be with an abstract ideal, and how distressed he can be with its concrete application. The call to improve the human race is often answered with enthusiasm, while the nocturnal cry of the baby in the next room is met with drowsy inertia. But this inconsistency has most serious implications when benevolence toward mankind is called "love," and when the avoidance of responsibility toward individuals is called "exercising one's rights".

Love is a tendency towards the real. Mankind, being an abstraction, is not real. The only legitimate sense in which mankind can be served is as a collectivity of individuals, each of whom awaits concrete reception of the personal touch of love. The problem of extending love properly to each human being is solvable in terms of justice.

No one is capable of loving every other individual person in a passionate way. Nor is anyone capable of loving mankind as an abstract idea. The former makes too great a demand on the lover; the latter lacks a substantial object of love. It is possible, however, to love some people in a very deeply personal way, while extending to others a form of love which is neither emotionally taxing nor devoid of objective substance. This form of love is called justice. Justice, then, is the expression of love on a universal level to each participant of the human race. Love unpaired with justice may foster favoritism, prejudice, or partisanship; justice unpaired with love may deteriorate into mere duty, casuistry, or legalism. Thus, unless justice and love are welded together, neither can be realized. The reason that idealistic love for mankind can be so dangerous is that when love and justice are separated, each is vitiated and neither is served. When love is united with justice, the value of the individual person is not lost in the blinding glare of idealism. Nor is it diminished by the existence of different forms of love.

One may wonder why one is attracted to a false love for mankind rather than to a realistic justice-linked love for individual men. For one reason, it is easier to be attracted to an ideal than to make the effort to discover what is good in each person. It is simply more convenient to see mankind as a monolith rather than as the multiplicity of individuals who constitute mankind. A more pernicious reason is that mankind as an idea resides in the mind, where it can ripen into an object or narcissistic ego attachment. Since the *idea* of mankind is largely the product of one man's limited imagination, one can easily shape this idea according to his own subjective preferences. One's idea of mankind, and therefore his ideas of what is good for mankind, may bear little resemblance to what individual men actually are and what they really need.

The preference for one's idea of mankind over existing men is a preference for egoism over realism. There is no truth in egoism, no reality in its inspiration, no love in its inception, and no justice in its execution. To love men properly and to serve them justly presupposes some knowledge of who they are in themselves, not as they are ideally perceived in some preconceived notion of mankind.

The philosopher-theologian Stanley Hauerwas writes:

> For there can be no love without respect, and respect must be built on a perception of the other's right of existence as he is, not as he has worth for me.

In order to reach a plane of love and justice, man must transcend egoism. The enormous effort so required explains the rarity of genuine human love and justice. Man's idea of mankind is unavoidably deficient. One has a basic option in his possible attitudes to his fellow men: 1) either he can claim to love them but will sacrifice certain individuals in accordance with his assumption of what is best for mankind in general; 2) or he can make no initial claims but can seek to recognize who men actually are and to help them toward the fuller realization of what nature gave them a right to enjoy.

In the former attitude there is neither love nor justice but instead the expropriation of human beings to an ill-founded egoism. In the latter attitude there are both love and justice, realistically based and projected through a regard for the individual's right to exist and to develop the positive endowments that are his birthright.

A good deal of the current pro-abortion argumentation assumes that love for mankind is superior to love for one individual. In other words, the life of the foetus should yield to a weightier consideration — the good of society. Whenever it appears that the continued existence of the foetus may interfere with the common good, that foetus should be sacrificed. Proabortionists thus pridefully point to their humanitarian concern for the whole of society.

This line of argumentation is spurious, because, as was explained above, mankind as such does not exist except as an *idea* and therefore cannot be an object of love. Ideas cannot be objects of love, because they cannot respond to love, share it, or benefit from its salutary powers. Mankind remains unaffected by all the wishful thinking and eager resolve that a man can muster.

Some scientists argue that a foetus carrying a deformed gene should be aborted. Allowed to live, they contend, he only further contaminates the human genetic pool. But they are concerned over something that cannot be suffered by any one person, for the "gene slum", as it is sometimes called, is not located within any particular individual or in any particular place. Mankind's gene pool can be understood only as an idea.

On the other hand, death by abortion is suffered by an individual person; it is something which substantially affects his real existence. Must individual lives be sacrificed in order to give certain people more pleasant thoughts about the human genetic pool? The futile love for mankind as an idea, as opposed to an effective love for men in particular, leads to just such distortions.

Moving from abortion to infanticide, Dr. James D. Watson, Nobel prizewinning geneticist, advocates that legal human status be withheld up to two days after the birth of an infant in order that "undesirable babies may be fished out of the gene pool." But who are the beneficiaries in this case? Not the babies, they are dead. Not the gene pool, it does not have concrete existence. Only a person can be a beneficiary because only a person can say "thank-you."

—15—

RAPE AND ABORTION: THE LOSS OF FAITH; THE DEATH OF THE MORAL IMAGINATION

Faith, it has been remarked, means believing in the sun even when it's not shining; in love even when you don't feel it; in God even when He's silent.

Faith is a spiritual strength which sustains us when what ordinarily gives us tangible support is not experienced by the sense. Through faith, what is physically absent becomes spiritually present. Faith activates our vital spiritual centers in the absence of their objects so that we can possess these objects in a more intimate and profound way. Without faith we become dependent on the moment. The absence of faith proves that our past experiences have left us no surviving legacy of strength, no inspiration to believe after the sense encounter has subsided. Faithlessness means the failure to commit real values to our heart.

And yet faith can be so lonely, whereas the sensuous experience of reality can be so comforting and consuming. For it is all too easy to forget the power of love and the pleasures of beauty. Whenever I return to Niagara Falls, I re-appreciate its grandeur and awesomeness, refresh myself with the actuality of the spectacle, and remind myself how inadequate the memory and imagination are as substitutes for the experience of the real.

We easily forget, too, the good of goodness and the banality of evil. Whenever I observe an act of kindness or generosity, I note how positive and creative goodness is and promise myself to remember how superior it is to evil.

Life is difficult; oftentimes our hopes are infected with gloomy discouragement. But life would be unbearable and our hopes destroyed if we thought that hate were stronger than love, deformity more real than beauty, evil more powerful than good, error more persuasive than truth. To accept life with hope and courage means to believe in the supremacy of love, beauty, goodness, and truth over their adversaries of hate, deformity, evil, and error. To have faith means to possess, spiritually, the positive and enduring values of existence as an inner source of strength in times of difficulty.

A moral person is one who lives with the faith that these positive values of love, beauty, goodness, and truth are more real and enduring than their opposites, and who makes his moral decisions in their favor. He finds them both a guide for authentic living and a key to life's existential meaning.

Without faith a person is disposed to be overcome by the confusion of the moment. He is inclined to be a slave to time's fancy, a pawn to the *Zeitgeist,* a helpless victim of fleeting sense experiences. Without faith he risks submitting to the mood of the present, whether good or bad. Old experiences cannot be relived, but they can be honored by the faith that survives them — the faith which keeps their value and reality close to the heart as a shield against future temptations. This kind of faith is indispensable for the moral life.

But in addition to faith, a moral life requires the use of a moral imagination. The moral imagination enables us to see, in a particular situation, how love may be expressed, truth served, goodness employed, and beauty restored. The moral imagination allows us to imagine a better world, because it is enlivened by a faith that such a world is possible. It is the link between moral intention and moral execution, connecting general values to particular, unique, moral situations. In its absence one tends to choose the path of least resistance, the societally conditioned response, the solution of visionless expediency.

The moral imagination is the child of faith in a way that faith is the child of experience. Faith retains and honors values which are derived from real experiences. The moral imagination discovers a way, inspired by faith, of returning those values to reality in the form of moral action. Faith preserves and the moral imagination enacts. To discourage the development of faith and the employment of the moral imagination is to demoralize man and entrap him within the confines of a set of mechanical responses to momentary experiences.

The following paragraphs present a consideration of how faith and the moral imagination are applicable to the particular moral situation created by a pregnancy which has resulted from forcible rape. The moral question centers around the morality of an induced abortion.

Rape is an evil of such magnitude that it threatens to overwhelm both the victim and her sympathizers. One of the most destructive aspects of evil is precisely its power to discourage by making goodness appear weak and fragile in comparison. Rape which results in pregnancy is the kind of evil that seems to transmit itself over an indefinite period of time. Abortion may seem a way of ending the transmission of that evil. But it is a submission to evil rather than a triumph over it. It is an admission that evil is stronger than goodness and love. For abortion itself is an evil. It is a violent strike against innocent life at a moment when faith in life and goodness is obfuscated by the shock of evil. The aggressive attack against the life of the unborn is a gesture consistent with the mentality of the rapist himself. Abortion means not only the loss of faith in the power of love and goodness but also the bankruptcy of the moral imagination.

In a crucial and dramatic situation, we ought to enlist those values in which we have the greatest faith. To invoke hatred of life, and violent aggression upon the unborn, betrays a greater confidence in evil, rather than goodness, as a remedy.

In baseball, a crucial and dramatic situation may call for lifting a weak hitter for a pinch hitter. The pinch hitter is the one in whom the manager has the greatest confidence in that particular situation.

When a woman has been impregnated through rape, her condition is treated in accordance with what is most fervently believed. Offering abortion indicates a belief in hatred, aggression, and evil. Offering love, support, guidance, and reassurance as positive alternatives indicates a belief in reverence and goodness.

In legalizing abortion in the case of rape, society places its confidence in hatred and evil as pinch hitters for love and goodness. It has forgotten, in the grip of the anxiety brought by the evil of rape, that goodness *is* the stronger remedy. Any legislation based on the conviction that evil is stronger than goodness and that faith in love is naive must necessarily have a demoralizing effect on society. It is *so* easy to destroy and *so* difficult to create. If creation were not more powerful and enduring than the forces of destruction, the human race would have long since perished. Abortion is ultimately a confession of faithlessness in the enduring positive values of reality. Therefore, it inevitably precedes distress, disillusionment, desperation, and despair.

In the movie "They Shoot Horses Don't They?", the girl who requested her own extinction was distraught and desperate. Her moral imagination had ceased to function. The 'friend' who pulled the trigger chose the simplicity of death over the challenge of life, the silence of unconsciousness over the voice of the moral imagination.

The simplicity of death by abortion hinders development of the moral imagination. Abortion is an expedient solution, not an imaginative or realistic one. With faith in enduring values and the functioning of the moral imagination, the power of love can counteract and surmount the evil of rape. The admonition not to be overcome by evil but to overcome evil by good suggests the only realistic basis for optimism. It is realistic because it represents faith in the power of the positive, optimistic because it represents faith in the eventual victory of goodness.

The ability to recognize and to love that which is good in the face of great injury is precisely the kind of strength which renews hope and offers a way out of a world broken by sin and shaken with doubt. Booker T. Washington once said:

> I shall allow no man to belittle my soul by making me hate him.

If such a remark could be part of the living philosophy of a man who, because of his color, was the constant object of hate, injustice, and derision, there is hope for us all. And especially there is hope that the woman impregnated through rape will refuse to imitate her assailant's evil but keep her heart fixed on the valuable life within her, saying:

> I shall allow no influence, legal, paternal, or societal, to belittle my soul by making me abort the child that grows within me.

—16—

TIME
ON MY
HANDS

Arnold Gesell, in his remarkable book *The Embryology of Behavior,* published in 1945, writes that the lines in the hands of the foetus have already been engraved by the eighth week of gestation. In addition to being a physiological marvel, the lines in the foetus's palm speak eloquently for his natural and indelible claim to his own unique future.

Aristotle called the hand "the organ of organs". The Latin word for hand — 'manus' — is the source of the word 'man'. The hand has an unusually rich symbolism in the history of Western thought. It displays the ring of fidelity as well as the mark of toil. It symbolizes prayer, friendship, greeting, honor, oath, love, tenderness, work, respect, farewell, stigmata. It has regal grandeur ("The hand that rocks the cradle rules the world") and moral implication ("the helping hand").

Yet the earliest and perhaps most significant meaning of the hand is offered at eight weeks by the foetus. In disclosing at so tender an age the lines of his palm, which will remain a distinctive feature throughout his life, the foetus symbolizes time compressed into a moment and a moment foretelling time. These permanently etched lines attest to the unbroken duration which unites the unborn with the adult. The foetus has time written on his hands — his time and his future life.

The foetal hand is but a symbol of time, and between the symbol and the reality it is easy for one to lose his way. Yet the foetal hand reminds us to reflect on the nature of time long enough to observe that, with regard to living things especially, time is in indivisible continuum, an unshrinkable duration, an unbroken transmission.

The contention that the human foetus is too undeveloped to be worthy of legal protection and human consideration is based on the fallacy that his lifetime is decomposable. To say that an infant is more human than an unborn foetus is to conceive of life as a series of stages, each one existing outside the other. Such a conception presupposes that the arbitrary temporal measurements which distinguish one stage of external development from another coincide with the real inner development of the organism. This is equivalent to thinking that the sun makes sixty separate and discrete movements per minute because the clock measures sixty seconds in a minute. In reality things do not move by a number of stop-and-go pulsations, although measurements by discrete numbers tend to create this impression. Numbers, measurements, stages of development, arrest the life-flow of an organism at a given moment. They unnaturally extract a moment out of its living duration and treat it, now dead and abstract, as if it were alive and concrete.

Investigations into the reality of time in the 20th Century have brought forth some of the most exciting conclusions ever reached by the human mind. Since the fall of classical physics with the introduction of Einsteinian relativity, it has become increasingly apparent that time is a real and inseparable part of the four-dimensional space-time continuum. Sir Arthur Eddington writes:

> I think we might go so far as to say that time is more typical of physical reality than matter.

In his book, *The Universe and Dr. Einstein,* Lincoln Barnett writes:

> The world *is* as space-time continuum; all reality exists both in space and in time, and the two are indivisible.

Teilhard de Chardin states a similar view:

> Time and space are organically joined again so as to weave together, the stuff of the universe. This is the point we have reached and how we perceive things today.

It is no longer accepted in modern science, nor in modern philosophy or even modern art, that anything can be understood apart from time. Space itself, let alone anything within space, cannot be understood apart from time. According to psychiatrist Viktor Frankl, man finds meaning in his life in terms of future goals, things to live *for*. There is no such thing as a moment, cut from the flow of time, which can be examined for itself. Nature does not exist in the moment, the philosopher Alfred North Whitehead reminds us. "Each phase in the genetic process", he writes, "presupposes the entire quantum." Psychologist William James pointed out many years ago that even the act of perception takes time. There is no perception of the instant. Everything in reality, to be seen in reality's terms, must be seen as process, involved inextricably with time and engaged in a dynamic, on-going movement.

One of the most significant philosophers of this century, Martin Heidegger, carefully explains in his major work, *Being and Time,* that time must be regarded as the horizon for the understanding of Being. "Man", he writes, "is always infinitely more than what he is at any given moment." Man is essentially a temporal creature whose past and present are dynamically projected toward a future.

Organisms do not grow to a certain point, like a line on a graph, and then stop, having nothing to do with what proceeds from them. There is, in Henri Bergson's terms, a "continuity of interpenetration in time, irreducible to a mere instantaneous juxtaposition in space."

The foetus is not, in reality, simply a foetus. Since he is inseparably united with time, time-flow, and his life-time, he is what he is destined to continue to be and become. To measure a human being only up to his first eight weeks and then decide that he is too young to be considered a real human being, is as unrealistic and incomplete an evaluation as measuring a person only up to his ankles and then deciding that he is short. To be fair and complete one must measure a person's height from his toe to his crown; one should measure *all* of his height. Likewise, to be fair and complete, one should measure *all* of an individual's time — from conception to natural death. Then one is in a most favorable position to understand the meaning and nature of that being. One should give the foetus *all* his time instead of unrealistically fractionalizing time down to a few weeks as if time itself were decomposable.

There is much wisdom in Heidegger's assertion that to philosophize is to learn how to wait. We cannot understand the mmeaning or nature of a being unless we wait for its value to unfold before us in time. A willingness to wait is also necessary if we are to understand and possess ourselves. "Through patience man possesses his soul" (Luke 21:19).

There is a disturbing impatience about the technology that seeks to reduce time to nothing. To see the foetus in space, take his height, foreclose his time, and commit him to the realm of the legally unprotected, discredits not only time but reality. The foetus from eight weeks on extends two delicately etched hands in an appeal for a future which is his. In these hands perhaps the symbolism and the reality do come together. As the poet T.S. Eliot has written:

Time present and time past
Are both perhaps present in time future.

17

FREEDOM AS A ONE-EYED JACK

When it comes to cards, I am a militant non-participant. There is something about the cabalic secretiveness and cultic seriousness which haunts a card game that I find personally uninviting. But I do have pleasant memories of spending long summer days as a youth playing back-porch poker. Deuces were always wild, then, and quite often so were jokers, red queens, mustachioed kings, aces, spades, and one-eyed jacks. By our mere agreement, the face value of any card could be transformed into that of any other card a player might hold. In our naivete we felt that each player's chance of winning was improved the more wild cards there were. Not understanding that poker is really a game of psychology, we approached it as an experience in freedom. However, our delusion was not complete; we knew better than to make everything wild. Some 'tame' cards had to be left in the deck. There had to be some restrictions if the game were to have any meaning. Besides, there had to be a way for a player to win occasionally with less than five aces.

Our poker rules illustrate the moral principle that freedom alone is emptiness and purposelessness. Hyde Partnow comments succinctly:

> I am free
> Not because I can fly
> But because I can touch
> The earth with my feet.

A friend once told me that if she could return to this world in another form it would be as a bird. The bird has always been a symbol of freedom. Yet even a bird in flight meets with opposition. Philosophers used to speculate that in an airless medium a bird would be able to fly faster. The truth is, of course, that in an airless medium a bird, not having anything on which to rest its wings, could not fly at all.

Freedom and restriction were born twins. Nonetheless, some people find it difficult to accept this truth. For them, freedom and restriction oppose one another, the former a blessing and the latter a curse. They judge moral restraints such as the Ten Commandments as delimiting freedom. Freedom and restriction may, in certain cases, oppose one another. But freedom enjoys purpose and direction only in a context of restriction. Thus, the true lover of freedom is just as ardent a lover of restriction.

A pianist does not desire another pair of hands or a keyboard twice the normal length. He is happy to develop his art within a narrow set of limiting conditions. The loving husband does not want more than one wife. His inclusive conjugal fidelity to one is also his exclusive conjugal restraint from others. When ballplayers accept foul lines, they accept foul and fair territory equally. When serious players sit down at a card table, they agree upon the face value of each card with exactly the same resignation. Divorcing restriction from freedom results in a loss of substance; a lack of direction. By attempting to achieve everything one achieves nothing.

Extreme permissiveness is a state in which all restrictions have been removed and everything is 'wild'. It is a state in which any act receives any name. Thus, abortion for convenience is called "therapeutic", "a child's right not to be born", "love", "post-conceptive planning", "fairness to the child", and so on. Refusing to perform an abortion is called "immoral", "criminal", "unjust", "irresponsible", "selfish", and so on. Adultery is termed "flexible monogomy", "playing around", "swinging", or "participating in adult games". Fidelity to one's spouse is termed "frustration", "selfishness", "being square", or "sexual inhibition". Where "fair is foul, and foul is fair", it is not surprising that moral bewilderment is so prevalent. Pure freedom means that anything is anything. It means that there is no solidarity to get in the way of things to give them definite shape and meaning. Things are named not by what they are but by how they are desired.

But extreme permissiveness, far from being an unadulterated blessing, fails to permit even the recognition of reality. To recognize reality one must learn to see the duet in things. Life is a dialectic. In its authentic form it arises between the poles of life and death, hope and discouragement, plan and compromise, achievement and surrender, intention and sacrifice, purpose and spontaneity, freedom and restriction. Chesterton put it this way:

> Rigidity that slightly yields, like Justice swayed by Pity, is all the beauty of earth. Everything seeks to grow straight; and happily, nothing succeeds in so growing. Try to grow straight and life will bend you.

Grace is the gentle glory of the bow bending without breaking, the man working without exhaustion, the woman sacrificing without complaint. It does not exist apart from harmonious duality.

Those who argue that women must be given the freedom to choose whether or not they should have an abortion are asking that we abandon this harmonious duality and play the game of life with all values wild. By this formula no one can win. We must recognize and understand what is written on the face of abortion, and act accordingly. The myth of the absolute value of pure freedom lures us away from reality and destroys creativity. Torn from its natural companionship with restriction, freedom becomes a form of sterile singularity. Unfettered freedom belongs to the realm of the imagination, where the idle fancier dreams of fountains of youth, elixirs of life, and Shangri-Las shorn of the realities of tooth, claw, fret, pain and — substance.

Man profits from his freedom only when he embraces its limitations, just as the bird flies only when it beats its wings against the resisting air. A human life is improved morally not through the avoidance of restrictions but through the utilization of the freedom defined by those restrictions. Pregnancy is a restriction. But it is one which helps to define how a woman can freely direct her love.

18

THE
BLAND
SAMARITAN

One virtue which the Good Samaritan had the good sense to possess was the ability to respond promptly to another's needs without first getting permission. Of course, the victim who was left half-dead by the roadside was hardly in a position to grant or withhold permission, but the Samaritan could have played things cozy for himself, as the priest and the Levite had done before him, by unobtrusively slipping past the beaten traveller on the other side of the road. Some sober reflections on the possible social repercussions of a Samaritan's caring for a Jew easily could have submerged his neighborliness. In modern times so many imitators of the Good Samaritan have been sued for practicing medicine either without permission or without a license that New York State, to cite one example, has passed a "Good Samaritan Law" to protect anyone acting in the esteemed tradition of the New Testament's good neighbor. Another reflection which could have caused the Samaritan to suppress his charitable instincts is that unless he first obtained permission to care for his helpless neighbor, he might later be accused of imposing his moral values. Today many Christians hesitate to respond to the needs of the helpless human in the womb for fear of imposing their values. The foetus, like the abandoned victim in the parable, is in no position to grant or withhold permission, but some Christians prefer to tip-toe past him along their own road of private concern.

The Good Samaritan, who for the Christian epitomizes the good neighbor, knew the difference between ministering to essential human needs and imposing arbitrary personal values. One cannot *impose* justice, mercy, and kindness on another — these values ought to exist between people. They fulfill neighborliness because they complement the essential needs of human nature. When the Christian defends the foetus's right to life, he is no more imposing a value than he would be in deterring a person from suicide or giving someone artificial respiration. Values may be said to be imposed only when they do not correspond to an essential human need.

The distinction between ministering and imposing is based on the distinction between first-order essential human relationships, which are natural, and second-order conventional human relationships, which are negotiable. The former do not require permission; the latter frequently do. One should not feel that he is imposing cheerfulness when he bids another an unsolicited good-morning: but he may be imposing gloom when he requires another not to be cheerful. One does not need permission to practice charity, but he should not paint his neighbor's house without first getting permission.

Pro-abortionists, in trying to dissuade defenders of the unborn from "imposing" values of justice, mercy, and kindness, speak as though there were no first-order essential human relationships and consequently no essential human needs that could be ministered without permission. But there are certain things which people must do without permission; the silence of the foetus makes that quite clear.

In a world of pure conventionality, filled with requisition forms, order blanks, permission slips, traffic signs, union rules, community by-laws, and legal contracts, a person may hesitate to perform any social action on his own, feeling that it must first be cleared by some duly appointed authority. In this kind of world the Good Samaritan is replaced by the Bland Samaritan who avoids his moral responsibilities to others by hiding under mountains of red tape, or by camouflaging them with painted layers of protocol, civility, and propriety.

> I should have been a pair of ragged claws
> Scuttling across the floors of silent seas.

T. S. Eliot's timid crab is an apt metaphor for the modern man who encapsulates himself within a shell of moral privacy, thus forfeiting the experience of sharing his humanity with others for the unsatisfying experience of mere observation. He has banished the danger of imposing his values on anyone else, but at the price of imposing a moral straight-jacket on himself.

George Szell, the late conductor of the Cleveland Symphony Orchestra, used to tell the following anecdote to reveal the difference in mentalities between Europeans and Americans: A European and an American, being led by St. Peter to their eternal rewards, reached a crossroad whose signpost read: right, to Heaven; left, to a lecture on Heaven. The European chose Heaven and the American took in the lecture.

Americans' preference for the vicarious, their willingness to forego their own experiences for the privilege of observing someone else's, has made them a nation of spectators. Girl watching, TV watching, film watching, window shopping, and sports spectating are national pastimes. For some people "realism" is something which unfolds only on celluloid; "live" means nothing more than an untaped performance. Kierkegaard once likened modern society to a group of theater spectators who applauded the repeated announcements that the building was on fire. Preferring the vicarious over the real can lead to the loss of the ability to distinguish one from the other.

In applauding the announcement of the fire, the theater-goer confesses his non-involvement with reality and his preferred absorbtion with that in which he has no part. The thirty eight witnesses to the rape and murder of Kitty Genovese in Kew Gardens, N.Y., failed to come to her rescue, according to their testimony, because they did not want to get involved. These thirty-eight people obviously preferred to remain in their own encapsulated, private worlds from which certain moral exigencies could be conveniently excluded.

The Good Samaritan was able to act morally without seeking permission because he was more than a spectator in life — he was a participant. The charge that defending the unborn is imposing one's values is really an invitation to vicarious living through spectatorship.

In the most lopsided college football game ever played, Georgia Tech defeated Cumberland College, 220-0. On one play, Cumberland quarterback, George Allen, fumbled the ball, and as three Georgia Tech ogres moved toward it, another Cumberland player politely got out of the way. Allen yelled to his teammate, "Pick it up". The player replied, "Pick it up, hell, I didn't drop it."

When a football player becomes a spectator in the very game in which he is supposed to be participating, a 220-0 loss becomes easier to understand. When other human beings become spectators to the very essential human needs with which they should be involved by nature, society must lose.

Modern indifference to the essential human needs of the unborn creates the Bland Samaritan, who cannot rest until he converts life participants to his form of moral privacy. His ideal is to exemplify the motto of "the bland leading the bland".

The person who waits for permission before responding to the moral needs of another has replaced his heart's natural inclinations with a set of arbitrarily assigned conventions. He is representative of a class of people C. S. Lewis called "Men without chests". Abortion is not a 'gut' issue, but an issue of the heart. "Men without chests" assume that the unborn are without rights. Their logic is consistent, but its spirit is heartless. Thought without feeling, logic without heart, fragments the world and estranges its inhabitants until there can arise no Good Samaritan because there are no longer any neighbors.

IV

A GLIMPSE OF THE TRANSCENDENT

"There are moments of silent depth in which you look on the world-order fully present. Then in its very flight the note will be heard; but the ordered world is its indistinguishable score. These moments are immortal, and most transitory of all; no content may be secured from them, but their power invades creation and the knowledge of man, beams of their power stream into the ordered world and dissolve it again and again."

— Martin Buber

—19—

PREGNANCY: THE PEACE MOVEMENT WITHOUT PEER

A few Springtimes ago, when the peace movement on the campus of a New York City university was in full flower, I thought I'd undertake a private survey to learn as much as I could from my peace-energized students about the nature of that elusive ideal which had so enthralled and unified them. Having contracted a mild case of peace-fever myself, I was prepared to allow my students to administer to me a booster shot. At the time, I had just begun teaching three divisions of philosophy with about fifty students in each class. The question I put to them was a model of brevity and, ostensively, a paragon of simplicity: "What is peace?" Immediately, a flurry of answers came forth: "Peace is the absence of war;" "Peace is freedom from turmoil;" "Peace is the avoidance of hostility;" "Peace is the removal of stress;" etc. The first 'peace offerings' were all phrased in the negative. The students were well prepared to tell me what peace wasn't. I suggested to them that defining peace negatively could lead to confusion and even to possible dissension within the ranks.

Look at the confusion and dissension brought about between the sexes as a result of the historical conception of a 'woman' as not a man and 'fe-male' as not a male. Plato had called woman a small man. Aristotle once referred to her as a castrated man. Freud saw her as envious of man because she wasn't a male. One writer quipped, "She's not much but she's the best other sex man has." Small wonder that Simone de Beauvoir, the intellectual matriarch of today's women's liberation movement, titled her study on the subjugation of the female *The Second Sex*.

Apprised and convinced of the dangers of defining peace negatively, the students began to strain for a positive rendition. "Peace is a state of Nirvana," one student said. "Peace is a condition of feelinglessness," offered another, "Peace is the cessation of pain," ventured a third. What was unsuitable about

100

these attempts at getting to the nature of peace, I responded, was that they were not distinguishable from 'Requiescat in Pace' or death.

A new specification must be added to any meaningful understanding of peace, I advised. Not only must peace be something positive, but it must be alive. Wishing to avoid identifying their peace movement with a collective death wish, my students then struggled to produce a statement on peace that was both positive and imbued with life. Alas, none was forthcoming. Realizing that asking for an academic, abstract understanding of peace was perhaps too much, I decided to make the question a little more practical, a little more existential. "What would you do if you wanted to find peace?" No answer. "Suppose, as an assignment, you were to experience ten minutes of peace within the next week. What would you do to savor that ten minutes of peace?" After a long pause, one girl confessed rather disconsolately, that given all the school assignments she was burdened with and all the deadlines she had to meet, finding peace was out of the question for at least several weeks.

Of the approximately one hundred fifty students I interrogated, not one could offer me the most meagre description of peace that was phrased positively in a manner which connoted life. I had thought that perhaps one at least would have paraphrased the old Augustinian notion that "Peace is the tranquility of order." Those interested in modern thought might have been counted on to offer a variant of the British philosopher Alfred North Whitehead's description of peace as "a trust in the efficacy of beauty."

It was a gloomy thought, but was it possible that 'peaceniks' in the thick of the peace movement didn't have any real insight into the nature of peace? Could it be true that the horror of war was so vivid in their minds that it displaced any positive sense of peace? Was peace a form of anaesthesia for them? The word tranquility, which is nearly synonymous with peace is usually heard in the cognate form of tranquilizer. Could there be a connection, then, between peace and narcotizing drugs? At any rate, it was clear that the forces which threatened to remove peace (war, pain, stress, hostility, etc.) loomed larger in their imaginations than the positive and active blessings which peace conferred. The meaning of Spinoza's words, "Peace is not the absence of war: it is a virtue born out of the strength of the heart," seemed so alien to their eager spirits which were bent on weeding the world of obstacles so that peace would be free to flower.

It seems reasonable to suggest that if any peace movement is to have serious and realistic results, it should draw its main inspiration from the positive and active content of peace rather than from a desire to avoid what appears to be inimical to peace. A man falls in love with a woman not because he fears loneliness but because he discerns something good and lovable about her. The best motive for learning is not a fear of ignorance but a love for truth. What are needed today, in order to help guarantee a measure of success to any peace movement, are clearer, more lively, more human and more positively compelling symbols of peace. Without symbols of peace that are clear and accessible, it is easy to confuse, distort or misconceive the true nature of peace.

The two most forceful symbols of peace, to my mind, in this regard, are those represented by the saint and the mother-with-child. In both cases, the elements of order, tranquility, union, life, beauty, purpose and love exist in a pre-eminent way. The saint is at peace because of the consuming love which unites him with his *Thou,* his God. The child in the womb is at peace because of the intimate and all-sufficient union he enjoys within the body of his mother. But the saint, because he is hidden, unrecognizable or virtually non-existent, fails to provide a pervasive visible symbol of peace from which people at large could take inspiration.

This leaves the pregnant mother in the unenviable position of providing for the world its most powerful and pervasive symbol of human peace.

Ironically, in an age when the need for peace is paramount, another movement, antithetical to peace, has taken up its banner alongside the 'peace movement'. The women's liberation movement was formed for the expressed purpose of emancipating the woman from the confining roles of mother and housewife. To effect this emancipation it has been deemed expedient to remove legal and social barriers to abortion. Since contraceptives are not completely reliable, a woman should remain at liberty to terminate unchosen and, therefore, unwanted pregnancies. But in being so liberated, the woman is also freed from the sacred and inviolate bond she once enjoyed with her unborn. It is difficult to regard the pregnant woman as a significant symbol of peace if what she carries under her heart is nothing more than another organ of her own body. It is hard to see the transcendent implication of her pregnant state when the 'subhuman' growth within her can be arbitrarily extinguished at any time. It becomes next to impossible to perceive the dignity of pregnancy when, as is the case with a growing circle of people, the foetus is viewed as an 'accident' or 'blob of protoplasm' and his delivery into the world is judged as 'causing pollution' or 'adding to the population explosion'.

That the "peace movement" and women's "liberation movement" have much in common is amply testified by the ideologies of a significantly high percentage of their common members and leaders. But neither, apparently, has very much to do with either peace or liberation.

There is an old Jewish saying that "in the mother's body man knows the universe, in birth he forgets it." The union of the child with the mother is so intimate and proper (Otto Rank, the psychologist, called it a "paradise" for the child) that it is unimaginable that the child should be anywhere else. For nine months the child knows (in the most Biblical and most unifying sense of 'knowing') his proper place in the universe. Birth is a disruption. It is a violation of the deepest and most peaceful form of co-existence humanly possible. But the nine month period of receiving the imprint of peace down into the very core of his being has its lasting effect. The child in the world, having "forgotten" the universe, seeks to find it anew, actively, freely and consciously. He seeks to find a new peace through love so that this time he is united with another while he possesses himself.

Man surrenders his natural connection with another before birth for his cosmic connection after birth. Thus his prenatal period bears a cosmic implication. He is not a parasite. He is not a mere appendage of his mother, nor is he her possession. Neither does he fall totally within the purview of her will and sovereignty. He has a destiny of his own which is to be fulfilled through a love which is his own. Already within the womb, writes the Jewish philosopher Martin Buber, inscribed "as a secret image of desire," is "the yearning for the cosmic connection, with its true *Thou*."

If it were possible for man to arrive directly into the world as an independently functioning being, without having spent any time in peaceful and intimate prenatal harmony with his mother, it is rather doubtful that he would ever possess the inclination to search for peace and intimacy. Time in the womb prefigures life in the world. What is learned in the schoolroom of the womb is the profound significance of peace, union, love and intimacy. Without that elementary education where would anyone have learned the value of such things?

It is right that there should be peace movements. The taste of peace in the mother accounts for the thirst for peace in the world. It is right that there should be liberation movements. The freedom achieved through the disruption of birth means that man should use his freedom to recover peace through consciousness and love. Our age has lost the symbols of peace which could offer to us its positive and active value. If there is to be an honest and fruitful attempt to achieve peace, the dignity and beauty of the mother-with-child must be reinstated.

Abortion and easy access to abortion destroy not only the peaceful slumber of the foetus but all the hopes for future peace which were born within the womb. The genesis of all desire for peace is within the mother. To banalize pregnancy by regarding abortion as a neutral and private matter is to dry up the well-springs of peace. To deny the beauty and the eminently human character of that tranquil and orderly reciprocity which flows between the mother and her unborn child is to suppress the most universal, accessible and prodigious symbol of peace man has ever been granted the privilege to perceive.

We will continue to make war, and all peace movements will remain as unfulfilled velleities, as long as we make war on motherhood and the innocent harbinger of peace within her. Until the nine month peace movement which is pregnancy is discerned in all its rich and transcendent implication, there is little chance that a widespread peace can ever become reality.

To be an apostle of peace and a proponent of 'liberalized' abortion is a curious contradiction. It is the stance of the somnambulist, the unthinking romantic, the idealistic humanist. Abortion and peace exclude each other. The war on the unborn has been more pervasive and has claimed more lives than any other kind of war in human history.

Will and Ariel Durant, in their well known book *The Lessons of History,* have estimated that in the past 3,421 years of recorded history, only 268 years have been free of war. But there was a time of peace when a Babe in Bethlehem, a Prince of Peace was preparing for His advent into the world. To all the tumultuous and glorious arrivals He could have chosen, He preferred the quiet peace of a mother's womb. The serenity and joy with which His mother accepted Him was transmitted to the world about. The song of "Peace on earth toward men of good will" offered a new and real hope because a woman, in receiving a child, had brought God to the world.

The world cannot accept Christ or peace or love when it accepts abortion. The babe in the primal state of the womb brings us a message. It is a message from another world — from God. Abortion is the decision not to listen to God and to ignore His most convincing argument for peace.

20

ABORTION: LOVE OR PITY?

Man has two ways of feeling towards his fellow man. They are pity and love. Through pity, man shares in the suffering, wounded condition of his seemingly Godforsaken neighbor. Pity "is the feeling," writes James Joyce, "which arrests the mind in the presence of whatsoever is grave and constant in human sufferings, and unites it with the human sufferer." Through love, on the other hand, man rejoices in that which is good, noble, and beautiful in another. Love, writes the Russian existentialist Berdyaev, is "seeing the other in God and affirming him in eternal life."

Love is greater than pity. Pity sees man in his desolation, his brokenness, his weakness as he stands alone without benefit of God's grace. Love sees man not only in his pitiable state but also in the context of the God who redeems him and the eternity which gives him meaning. Pity is therefore a part of love. Love contains pity but pity may exist without love. That is why one may be wary of pity. It can lead to love but it can also renounce God and destroy love; it may rise to love but it may also sink to the level of contempt. Man's pity for the wailing, agonizing fate of another can be so overwhelming that it may cause him to disdain, denounce, and deny God, as Nietzsche does in *Zarathustra* and Sartre in *Les mouches*. In contemning God, man thus rejects the love which must bear suffering. There are those who profess brotherly love who, in actual fact, possess nothing higher than contemptuous pity.

Some have persistently defended abortion on the basis of love for the unborn. There is no question that abortionists have pity for the unwanted, possibly deformed unborn whose advent in the world is so untimely and inopportune. In fact, their pity is no doubt a splendid virtue. Abortionist humanitarians are able to spread their doctrine so effectively because they appear so humane. Pity responds to one of the deepest needs in man. "Is there no pity sitting in the clouds, that sees into the bottom of my grief?" wrote Shakespeare. Only Hell is without pity. But it is indeed questionable to say that one's pity for the indigent unborn rises to the level of love when one advocates abortion. Pity can be a powerful and moving emotion. It can shake a man through and through until he cannot imagine there could be a higher and more deeply felt human emotion. Yet love remains, and it is superior to pity.

In an attempt to illuminate the purity of love against inferior human dispositions such as pity and prudery, which are sometimes mistaken for love, Kierkegaard offers an analogy in which he compares a genuine artist to a charlatan. One, who claims to be a genuine artist, speaks accordingly:

> I have travelled much and seen much in the world, but I have sought in vain to find a man worth painting. I have found no face with such perfection of beauty that could make up my mind to paint it. In every face I have seen one or another little fault. Therefore I seek in vain.

The other, who disclaims any title of artist, speaks of himself quite differently:

> Well, I do not pretend to be a real artist; neither have I travelled in foreign lands. But remaining in the little circle of men who are closest to me, I have not found a face so insignificant or so full of faults that I still could not discern in it a more beautiful side and discover something glorious. Therefore I am happy in the art I practise. It satisfies me without making any claim to being an artist.

Can there be any doubt that the latter is the true artist because he brings something with him to see the hidden beauty in others? The artist discerns beauty because he has the perception to see it. He preserves it in his art because he does not want it to escape the attention of others. The faults and imperfections he sees do not unsettle him because he sees the inner glory. The charlatan rejects his subject as soon as he locates an imperfection in it. He will not endure the ungainly aspect of the common face. He focuses on the fault and dismisses the subject as unfit for his art.

The one who pities the unborn but finds no reason to keep them alive has stopped short of love. The one who loves is the one who reaches through pain and misery to ignite an inner value which is worth preserving and promoting. In the dark and voiceless world of Helen Keller the loving touch of an Anne Sullivan evinced a meaning. Into the desolation of dying Indians, the loving smile of a Mother Teresa instills a hope.

The one who can only pity is overwhelmed and paralyzed by the fact of human suffering. The zealous humanitarians who pity without love are inspired by the illusion that it is possible to free the world altogether from suffering, to bring about an uninterrupted earthly beatitude. Malcolm Muggeridge has remarked that in all his days of world travelling, of visiting the sick and forsaken in the obscurest parts of the globe, he has never found humanitarians by the side of the hopeless suffering. Those who nursed the suffering were those who saw the light in Christ's suffering.

What makes suffering so unendurable, Nietzsche has said, is not the pain so much as the senselessness of it. The Christian, because of Christ, sees the redemptive sense in suffering and can embrace it with his love. Perhaps the essential task of the Christian is to alleviate the suffering without betraying the sufferer. This requires the lover to accept and even embrace suffering himself.

It is a superficial and erroneous criticism of Christians that they are masochistically attracted to suffering. The truth is that, although suffering is as abhorrent to them as to anyone else, the Christian can see through suffering. He knows its redemptive power and can live in hope, in spite of the human condition. He knows the Easter which follows Good Friday and "the tranquil blossom on the tortured stem." The pitying humanist can make no sense out of the human condition and a world of suffering. His only alternative is to remove suffering by destroying the sufferer.

Not only does the abortionist fail to love the unborn, despite the intensity of his pity for them, but in his shrinking from their disadvantaged condition, real or prospective, he actually seeks to destroy love. In a world where people are anaesthetized with drugs, TV, and easy chairs there is no need for love. But that "Brave New World" is inhabited only by the living dead and the patiently dying. It is Prufrock's world where man "measures out his life with coffee spoons." It is the Waste Land where there are "voices singing out of empty cisterns and exhausted wells," and "dry sterile thunder without rain." The abortionist does not see himself as part of the Waste Land because he has never found a love stronger than pain. His only concern is to make life comfortable; and in pursuing that noble aim, he succeeds only in desensitizing a feel for life. The abortionist performs his operation on himself.

21

HUMANICIDE
AS A VIABLE
ALTERNATIVE

The question of putting an end to the human race has never been given a fair hearing. Sporadic historical attempts at genocide have usually been so grim, unsuccessful and generally unpopular that the prospect for giving serious collective thought to the matter of exterminating all classes of humans has never come into vogue. However, in recent years, a widespread abortionist philosophy has supplied the nucleus for what is probably the best argument ever advanced in favor of humanicide.

Abortionists argue that foetal human life may be extinguished because of genetic defects or physical deformity, or because its unwanted status may dispose it to a life of uncertainty, rejection, and possible premature death. Essentially, the abortionists are arguing that a child may be aborted to spare him the pain and ignominy which attend his defectibility and mortality. A simple, logical extension of the abortionist philosophy makes the case for humanicide. Since we are all saddled with incurable defectibility and mortality, why not universalize the humanistic concern for the unborn so that everyone may be equally spared the ignominy of pain and the uncertainty of the hour of death?

The British political philosopher Thomas Hobbes once characterized man's life as "solitary, poor, nasty, brutish and short." Even today, this summary does not fall much short of the mark. Would it not be an act of heroic freedom, then, for man to resist the blind will that impels him to partake in the endless, meaningless cycle of life, misery, and death, and assert his independence by defiantly discontinuing such folly? Hamlet thought it a "consummation devoutly to be wished," before he lost his courage.

Leibniz, in the 17th Century, saw very clearly that the reason men disagreed and fought with each other was that they were allowed to think in the first place. He began work on a universal calculating machine that would solve all disagreements for man by securing international peace by dispensing with thought. Man was defectibile but his technical replacement need not be. Leibniz's insight was that if thinking causes disharmony, then disharmony can be avoided only by removing thinking.

In the present day, Pamela Mason's book, *Marriage is the First Step to Divorce,* presents a similar philosophy. Divorces, so painful and damaging, can be avoided only by repealing the institution which makes them possible — marriage.

This is precisely the thinking of the abortionist. The turbulent future of an unwanted child can be avoided by aborting him. By extension, all possible death and disability can be eradicated by discontinuing the human race. Humanicide is the permanent human triumph over defectibility and mortality. It is the avowed goal of every abortionist humanist who takes his philosophy to its logical extreme.

When Albert Camus opens his book *The Myth of Sisyphus* by stating, "There is but one truly serious philosophical problem and that is suicide," he is writing for an international audience, and the reasons he presents which make "dying voluntarily" plausible have universal application. While Camus reflects specifically on the plausibility of suicide, he is also presenting evidence for the cogency of humanicide. In saying that the "insane character of daily agitation, and the uselessness of suffering" may be swiftly terminated through suicide, he supplies the same basic reasons for humanicide that abortionists put forth in defense of abortion.

The logical weakness of genocide is its unevenness. The essential assumption of genocide is that life is good for one class of people but not good for another. Since all classes of people are grounded in the inescapable human condition that inevitably leads to disease and death, selective genocide is philosophically untenable. Legal abortion, as an instance of selective genocide, is therefore unsupportable. The only logically consistent attitudes which would respect the equality of human beings and their basic existential situation are either humanicide or some other attitude by which a meaning and value can be drawn from the human condition.

If men cannot endure an imperfect life that leads through pain and ends in death, then voluntary dying is a sensible way out of a senseless world. But if there could be a meaning to acceptance of such severe self-limitations, then there might be a reason to allow the human race to continue. If man could somehow learn to glory in his infirmity, perhaps life would be less absurd.

Some have argued that God offers meaning to man's imperfect life. A God, they suggest, who sought to give man happiness without at the same time abandoning him would withhold the gift of self-sufficiency in order to perpetuate man's need for Him. "No gift inspires affection," wrote George Bernard Shaw, "unless it is accompanied by the power to withhold." Or, in the words of Francis Thompson:

> All which I took from thee I did but take,
>> Not for thy harms,
> But just that thou might'st seek it in
>> My arms.

This theistic argument is an interesting one and is fundamentally opposed to the humanistic desire for human self-sufficiency or oblivion. The humanistic philosophy is essentially Godless, because it places all of its hopes in man. It is also essentially winless, because, in due times, all men must succumb to death. Atheistic humanists may postpone or hasten death but they cannot overcome it. In the final analysis, their ultimate contribution is not impressive, but at least it is their own:

> And the wind shall say: "Here were decent godless
>> people:
> Their only monument the asphalt road
> And a thousand lost golf balls." (T.S. Eliot)

—22—

ABORTION CHRISTIANITY AND DEICIDE

To the Orthodox Jewish mind, abortion on request and the prevention of the Messiah's entrance into the world are ideologically parallel. To Christian thinking, the expressions "no room in the inn", "no space in the womb", and "no place in the heart" are analogous. The meeting point of Orthodox Jewish and Christian thought is the belief in the Messiah coming into the world by being born of a woman; in heaven and earth coming together in the sanctuary of the womb. The basic point of disagreement which divides these two religions is not theological but historical. The Christian believes that Christ is the Messiah. The Jew awaits the Messiah's advent. Consequently, the Christian becomes more past oriented than the Jew in establishing the focal point of his religion. Since abortion bears upon the future, it might seem that the Jew is better disposed to see the connection between abortion and deicide. Nonetheless, the Christian perceives this connection quite clearly.

The revolutionary kind of love which Christ preached required His followers to love their neighbors as themselves and their enemies as their friends. This teaching was based on the principle that Christ was present in each person. Loving others, therefore, meant loving Christ: "Whatsoever you do for the least of My brothers, that you do unto Me." Conversely, withholding love from others was an offense against Christ. Love meant both the discovery of Christ and unification with Him. Had Christ not insisted that He be sought by men's loving men, Christians would have sought Him directly, and in so doing would have abandoned each other. But Christ remains hidden so that men don't ignore each other. The purity of Christ's love for men is revealed by His unwillingness to spotlight Himself and cast a shadow over the human race. Christ, whose love excludes jealousy, loves men in such a way as not to divert them from loving one another.

When the Christian neglects his responsibility to love the unborn human, he interrupts his search for Christ. If he denies the unborn their lovability, he ultimately must deny his own lovability in the eyes of Christ. The difference between an adult and an unborn child, no matter how striking it appears to be, is insignificant when compared to the difference that distinguishes man from God. The gap between man and God is the infinite, whereas the gap between adult and unborn is annulled by the passing of a few short years. If man cannot love his own, he cannot hope to be loved by his Creator.

To the Christian, abortion is a re-enactment of deicide. It slays the Christ who lies hidden in the mother's womb. Moreover, it tends to destroy the abortionist's faith that he could ever be loved by his own Father. Consequently, it tends to destroy the Christ who dwells within the abortionist himself.

Christ is constantly trying to break into the world. But He does not want to force His arrival on men. So He respects their will. Neither does He want to arrive so triumphantly and conspicuously that His presence would distract men from loving each other. So He comes into the world in the modest form of a babe, and waits hopefully for the will of the parents to say, "we accept you."

Heaven and earth meet in the mother's womb. Decisions concerning the fate of the unborn have, for the Christian, profound and far-reaching implications. The eternal struggle between Mary and Eve resounds in the heart of every pregnant mother. The will of Mary, who received Christ by saying, "Let it be done unto me according to Thy Word", is opposed by that of Eve, who seeks more to be God than to transmit Him.

The abortion debate is the test case for separating Christian thinking and practice from those of the anti-Christ. For the Christian who receives the child, life is exciting and full of promise because he has discovered how near at hand the kingdom of God can be. The pro-abortionist, when confronted with an unwanted pregnancy, is overcome by fear and shuts out God's entrance. He thinks that a better world can be organized without God.

Throughout the writings of the great Christian novelist Dostoevsky, one central insight is made clear time and again: "Man cannot organize the world for himself without God; without God he can only organize the world *against man*."

—23—

BIRTH AND DEATH: THE ROSE PALACE AND THE FIERY DRAGON

Anyone who has observed a plant grow from seed, mature, flower, and wither with the formation of its fruit, has witnessed the natural intimacy which exists between birth and death. The plant exhausts itself by emptying its substance into its fruit. The continuance of the species is thereby assured, but at the expense of the individual.

It is a biological truism that in the heart of Nature, coming into being and passing away are inseparable. "The cult of germination", writes Simone de Beauvoir, "has always been associated with the cult of the dead."

This force of Nature, with its drive toward the perpetuation of the species and its indifference to the fate of the individual, is keenly felt even on the human level. The German philosopher Hegel's dictum that, "The birth of children is the death of parents", is a revealing description of the sacrificial aspect of reproduction. One reason that motherhood is honored is that it represents such sacrifice. Seneca, the Roman stoic, lavished praise upon his mother for permitting him to be born. He understood how strong, in the pregnant woman, could be the temptation to abort in self-defense. In pregnancy, where the Will of Nature is so forcefully present, a woman may very well fear the loss of her life. She may fear its total loss in death, or its partial loss in the suffering, incapacitation, and powerlessness which are portents of death.

Abortion, seen in this light, is a heroic strike against the implacable necessity of Nature. A woman has an abortion to save herself — to release herself from the grip of death. Abortion is an attempt to defeat death, whose threatening face appears when there exists too close an involvement with the reproductive power of Nature. Abortion is a rational self-defense reaction against unchosen sacrifice. It is, in Schopenhauerian

113

terms, the choice that reason and *knowledge* might triumph over the blind and suffocating *will* of nature. It is a deliverance, from natural containment to spiritual freedom.

In a perfectly rational world, where suffering and death made no sense, abortion would be reasonable. Birth is what would be difficult to justify. Germain Greer's campaign in behalf of Women's Liberation for the reproduction of the ultimate contraceptive is a highly rational expression of the desire to be released from Nature and freed from death. The Pro-life argument that choosing abortion means choosing death, misses the mark. Pro-abortionists are very much against death — the death of the woman.

The desire to reject death and its prefigurements, suffering and sacrifice, is understandable. The instinct for self-preservation is both forceful and elementary. Furthermore, the desire to surmount death and all the shadows of death, is consistent with man's natural superiority to the finitude which circumscribes his mortal life. And yet this yearning for immortality, which marks man's excellence, is also a sign of his helplessness. Nothing is more vain than seeking to avoid death. "Many wonders there be, but nought more wondrous than man", wrote Sophocles, "yet for death he hath found no cure." Death may be resisted at every turn, but it remains an inevitability. The strongest will of nature's finest creature is powerless against the inexorable fact of death. In the words of Emily Dickinson:

Because I could not stop for Death
He kindly stopped for me.

A pregnant woman is intimately and substantially involved in the tension between the conflicting forces of birth and death. Human existence, under ordinary circumstances, develops in the broad life space that separates birth from death. Pregnancy dramatically unites these two poles, creating a dilemma which appears insoluble. To choose birth, the woman must accept sacrifice — a dying to oneself. To choose abortion and reject dying to oneself, the woman must choose an unattainable ideal — her own immortality. In choosing birth, she fails to maintain self-interest; in choosing abortion, she fails to secure self-interest. In purely rational terms the situation is irresolvable.

The solution to the dilemma involves breaking loose from an air-tight world of rational self-interest. A choice based on self-interest and death rejection is unsound, because death is unavoidable. It is unrealistic to live in fear of that which is unavoidable. Excessive concern for self-security can bring about increasing misery because it is a concern that can never be consummated. Paradoxically, if everyone always acted to protect himself against suffering or sacrifice, no one would ever have been born to worry about such a problem.

What we need is courage, especially the kind described by Paul Tillich in his book *The Courage to Be:*

> Courage is the readiness to take upon oneself negatives, anticipated by fear, for the sake of a fuller positivity.

Scholar Josef Pieper makes the following observation about the couragelessness, weakness, and ineffectiveness of acting primarily out of self-security:

> To the modern science of psychology, we owe the insight that the lack of courage to accept injury and the incapability of self-sacrifice belong to the deepest sources of psychic illness. All neuroses seem to have as a common symptom an egocentric anxiety, a tense and self-centered concern for security, the inability to "let go"; in short, that kind of love for one's own life that leads straight to the loss of life. It is a very significant and by no means accidental fact that modern psychology frequently quotes the Scriptural words: "He who loves his life will lose it."

Carl Jung puts the same observation more succinctly: "Neurosis is a substitute for legitimate suffering." Paul Tillich adds: "Neurosis is a way of avoiding being by avoiding non-being."

It is not unusual for people to expend so much energy in avoiding death that, in the process, they fail to live. A most dramatic instance of this appears in Henrik Ibsen's play *When We Dead Awaken*. Rubek, a sculptor, avoids what he fears will cause him to compromise his total commitment to art. He avoids love for his model, Irene. After a long separation from him, the disillusioned, dispirited Irene says to Rubek:

> "We only recognize the things we've lost, when — when we dead awaken."
>
> "And, then — what do we really see?", asks Rubek, shaking his head sadly.
>
> "We see that we have never lived", answers Irene.

The death which haunts the prison of neurotic self-interest cannot be overcome without the courage which is born of love. The recognition of self-transcending values cannot take place apart from the self-forgetfulness that courageous love engenders. And if one risks suffering, sacrifice, and even death for his love, then those risks but honor and glorify the splendor of that love. "Flame were not flame", wrote the poet Don Marquis, "unless it met the dark."

Pro-abortionists play on desire for self-security to rationalize both abortion and the avoidance of those sacrifices necessary for authentic living. Dr. Robert Hall, in his book *A Doctor's Guide to Having an Abortion,* discusses some of the "reasons" a girl may offer her doctor to persuade him of her need for an abortion. One of the "reasons" he suggests is "revulsion at the thought of changing another thousand sets of diapers." Under this kind of mentality, courage, love, and authentic living are optional values while the neurotic desire for self-security is an inalienable and fundamental right.

The reason that "it is better to have loved and lost than never to have loved at all" is that in spite of heartbreak, one has savored a life that, rising above the paralyzing concern of self-security, has united him in joy with the life and values around him. The happy, proud, memorable moments are those when man catches a glimpse of something more important than himself. But he never awakens to anything greater than himself unless he first loses himself. Only in accepting death is one ever born to life; only in accepting death does one give birth to life. Death is defeated when it is accepted through self-less, courageous love. The philosopher George Santayana writes:

> It may indeed be said that no man of any depth of soul has made his prolonged existence the touchstone of his enthusiasms. Such an instinct is carnal, and if immortality is to add a higher inspiration to life it must not be an immortality of selfishness. What a despicable creature must a man be, and how sunk below the level of the most barbaric virtue, if he cannot bear to live and die for his children. . . .

Those who argue that a woman has a fundamental right to an abortion are, in reality, seeking to split the marriage between birth and death established by Nature. However, what Nature has united, no man can tear asunder. They also seek to render superfluous the self-less and courageous love which alone can surmount death. However, life's moral verities cannot be neglected with impunity. Pro-abortionists are trying to find a way into a better life that bypasses death. But there is no such way. Pro-abortionists are seeking an illusion. They would like to enter the rose palace without having to slay the fiery dragon. Christ's words, "I have come to bring a sword, not peace", suggests the weaponry which must be used to slay the dragon. And the dragon is ourselves. "And the fire and the rose are one."

The fall doth pass the rise in worth;
For birth hath in itself the germ of death,
But death hath in itself the germ of birth.
It is the falling acorn buds the tree,
The falling rain that bears the greenery,
The fern plants moulder when the ferns arise.

For there is nothing lives but something dies,
And there is nothing dies but something lives,
Till the skies be fugitives,
Till Time, the hidden root of change, updries
Are Birth and Death inseparable on earth;
For they are twain yet one, and Death is Birth.

—FRANCIS THOMPSON

24

ME
AND MY
SHADOW

> Between the conception
> And the creation
> Between the emotion
> And the response
> Falls the Shadow

(T.S. Eliot)

As one pages through the limitless literature on abortion, he finds time and again, citations from women which identify their liberation with an escape from the tyranny of their bodies. One characteristic citation, from a woman who had just undergone an abortion, reads:

> I just could not allow myself to feel so much at the mercy of my biology. I was damned if I was going to let my body dictate the rest of my life.

This fear of bodily entrapment suggests that women's liberation may be a liberation from womanhood itself, a movement toward masculinity or perhaps toward that Margaret Mead has described as the "third sex".

Traditionally, woman has been regarded as substance, man as reflection; woman constant, man erratic. Karen Horney, among others, has remarked that men struggle so hard to prove their creativity because they envy the ability to give birth which belongs to woman alone. "The truth is," wrote Jean Guitton, "that the woman is more near the human than man, so easily estranged from what is human." The expressed desire to be estranged from one's own body has been more typical of the individious male than the mature woman. Hence, her claim that a woman has a right to control her own body may be a better indication of a personality disorder than a persuasive argumentation for relaxing abortion laws.

This split between a woman and her body signifies a kind of psychic division that would leave a woman alienated from herself. Of course, there is a legitimate sense in which the will should control one's actions. This implies self-control — using the word "self" to denote the whole person. But even here, the will cannot have control over its own primary ordination, it cannot determine its natural inclination toward happiness. However, stating that the woman must control her body suggests that the body is not an integral and authentic part of the woman. The woman who thus separates herself from her own body, as if it were some property she owned, disembodies herself, in effect. That is to say, she places her *self* as controller at a distance from her *body* as the object controlled. This form of disembodiment, usually associated with only the most insecure person, resembles the anxious male's struggle to emancipate himself from the burden of corporeality: Faust's ravenous hunger for liberating knowledge. Icarus's desire to fly, Origen's self-castration, Descartes' partition between soul and matter, Bertrand Russell's expressed preference for a world of pure mathematical though, and Sartre's disdain for the "obscene paste" of existence. Philosopher W.T. Stace provides an almost comical instance of such disembodiment in this remark: "I become aware of my body in the end chiefly because it insists on accompanying me wherever I go."

It is fairly common to come across the male who regards his body as a burdensome weight that restricts intellectual achievements by its incessant demands for food, exercise, rest, and relaxation. It is much more common to find in him a similar dichotomy between logic and feeling. For some men, it is a point of honor to follow their logic even when it is at odds with their feeling. Men often seek the logic of love as if love were to exist whole and entire on a rational plane.

The woman, on the other hand, who respires with the moon and is intimately linked with the natural tides of the cosmos, usually integrates her heart and mind. The sociologist Georg Simmel has pointed out that for woman, "Being and idea are indivisibly one." A woman is not so much illogical as capable of fusing logic and feeling into an indistinguishable unity. The charge that women are illogical arises from a male point of view in which logic is conceived as impersonal and objective.

Throughout the history of the West, wisdom (*Sophia*) has always been symbolized by the woman. It has been remarked that women are not great philosophers or composers but rather are incarnations of philosophy and music: *philosophia, musica,* and *femina* are one in substance. The man, because he is more detached from the bonds of nature, is better able to separate thought from feeling and idea from being, and thus intellectualize the world in philosophy and rhaposodize his love in art.

At the same time, in Western tradition, the individual woman's inability to bear children has been regarded as a tragedy. In *King Lear,* the ingratitude of his daughter Goneril enrages Lear, and in the white heat of his anger he pronounces the ultimate curse upon her:

> Hear, nature, hear; dear goddess, hear!
> Suspend thy purpose, if thou didst intend
> To make this creature fruitful:
> Into her womb convey sterility:
> Dry up in her the organs of increase,
> And from her derogate body never spring
> A babe to honour her!

That a woman should seek to gain control of her own body, writes Sidney Cornelia Callahan, ought to be an agreeable to the male mind, since "men are only too happy to separate female 'reproductive systems' from the self." The woman who conforms to a male norm, however, surrenders those virtues which honour and distinguish her womanhood — like the horse which learned how to sing like a nightingale but forgot how to whinny like a horse. The Freudian psychology of woman is an essentially male view that sees the woman as suffering chiefly from her deprivation of the male organ. Strict Freudians judge the woman negatively (from the standpoint of her not being a woman). The emancipation of the woman is bad, writes Berdyaev, "if it means the distortion of the eternal feminine, an attempt to imitate and to be a bad copy of man." That is, a woman makes an excellent woman but an inferior man.

One of the best-known examples of disembodiment and self-alienation in modern poetry is to be found in T.S. Eliot's "The Love Song of J. Alfred Prufrock":

> Let us go then, you and I
> When the evening is spread out against the sky
> Like a patient etherised upon a table;

According to Eliot scholars, Prufrock is a divided self. The "you" in the first line is the amorous, bodily, sexual self. The "I" is the timid, conscious self who fears the carnal and shuns the corporeal. "You" and "I" taken together make an incomplete person who has consciousness without love, thought without action. In fact, Prufrock desires the numbness and inactivity of the anesthetized patient.

Prufrock is the anxious, incomplete, divided, disembodied male estranged from himself, who becomes, oddly enough, a model for the woman who wants to control her own body. The woman who separates self from body, as Prufrock separates "I" from "you", lacks the integration to be spontaneous, creative, whole, and complete. A woman, of course, need not conceive in order to be complete, but she cannot deny herself, seek to overhaul herself, or, as Lady Macbeth put it, "unsex" herself, without rendering herself considerably less than complete.

The division of the "liberated woman" is reinforced and partially maintained by the technologies of contraception and abortion. Thus divided, and shielded from her biology, she then asks the same timid question Prufrock raises, "Do I dare disturb the universe?"

When the divided woman accidentally conceives, the shadow of fear falls between conception and creation. This is abortion. When sexual emotion is activated, the same shadow of fear falls between that emotion and the generous response of her whole being. This is contraception. In either case, made ambivalent by fear, divided by technology, incomplete by choice, the "liberated" female is not a woman, sound and unified, generous and giving. She is a counterfeit woman, one who prefers the divided self, the leap into darkness, the reproach of mature men, and the refusal of reality.

> Thou art sweeter,
> And upon Prufrock
> I will gild my perch;
> And the prates of Belles
> Will not bewail against it.

V

THE CLIMATE
OF
CULTURE

"We are bleeding at the roots, because we are cut off from the earth and the sun and the stars, and love is a grinning mockery, because, poor blossom, we picked it from its stem on the Tree of Life, and expected it to keep on blooming in our civilized vase on the table."

— D.H. Lawrence

25

MODERN FASTIDIOUSNESS: HAS IT MADE LOVE OBSOLETE?

The difference between major league baseball and the bush league variety is that in the majors, a ball is deemed unfit for play when it is merely scuffed, whereas in the bush leagues what is required to render the ball unplayable is little less than its total destruction. Affluence fosters fastidiousness. If you can afford a superfluity of baseballs, you can afford to be fussy about their condition.

Similarly, the rich man doesn't send his worn shoes to the cobbler. He discards them. Second hand cars are for people who travel the highways second class. Junkyards are graveyards to the wealthy but shopping marts to the poor. The rich throw out the worn, while the poor prolong its life through restraint and repair.

Antoine de St. Exupery wrote a story about a 'Little Prince' who, on some far-distant planet, cared for and protected what he believed to be the only flower of its kind in the universe. But when he arrived on earth and discovered that same flower flourishing by the thousands, he began to regret the time and devotion he had wasted upon his flower. Things become cheap when they are plentiful; they are not valued highly when they can easily be replaced.

In *Robinson Crusoe,* the reverse situation exists. The movement is from plenty to poverty. Crusoe finds himself alone on an island. He has rescued from a shipwreck a cache of goods, among them household utensils, hunting implements, working tools, and a Bible. None of these provisions are replaceable, and therefore he fully recognizes their value. Each item becomes an ideal of its kind and must not be lost. The challenge and the romance begin at this point. Crusoe must deal with his limited and indispensable treasure with caution, and restraint. His security will be measured not by wealth but by resourcefulness; his success will be assured not by status but by restraint. Ironically, on this island of solitude, made even narrower by a paucity of supplies, the qualities which begin to emerge in Robinson Crusoe are distinctly human. In his former home in England, having been dulled by education and pampered by society, Crusoe had not known the awakening experience of living life at the edge of peril. Now that he himself has been rescued from shipwreck, his existence becomes all the more precious. Having narrowly escaped oblivion, he finds his life suddenly endowed with a new meaning, and a value which elicits a new love. In his former affluent surroundings, his life had had less drama and the love which treasures life and cherishes each morning's sun had yet to be aroused.

In addition to fostering fastidiousness, affluence tends to render the human virtues of caution, restraint, care, concern, and even love unnecessary, or at least more difficult to come by. An affluent Crusoe would have made a dull story. As Chesterton has pointed out, "economy is far more romantic than extravagance."

Henry David Thoreau, who rediscovered his humanity after withdrawing to a wooded solitude, was convinced that freedom exists in proportion to the number of things man does not need to own. St. Francis of Asissi and Mahatma Gandhi are revered for their extraordinary ability to exemplify this kind of wantless life. Contentment is more easily found by looking for what is beautiful in everything than by fastidiously searching for perfection in anything. The virtues of the poor will win for man his humanity. To make do without much ado requires genuine humility. To find something of value in everyone and everything, as the saint sees Christ in the leper, or a George Washington Carver sees innumerable potentialities in the peanut shell, requires the vision of love.

There is growing social approval in North America for throwing a person out of the game of life at the first sign of a deformity. Can man afford to be so fastidious toward his fellow man? Can he remain blind to the value and lovableness of each person without destroying that value and lovableness in himself? Should society discount the unique value in each person and treat people as replaceable commodities? Some argue strenuously that parents should abort their deformed child and then try later to produce a more 'deform-free' edition. But when babies are used as replacements for other babies, then the vision of love has been replaced by the fastidiousness of affluence.

How difficult it is to win back the "dowry of good-nature, of love," wrote Kierkegaard, "when one is first initiated into the contamination of fastidiousness." To say, "you are not good enough for my love" is a judgment more against the parent than the child. The genius of love can always uncover the lovableness in man. Fastidiousness is weak because it has no vision, cannot search out hidden sources of beauty, knows nothing of patience, tolerance, and care. It is a form of ultra-Puritanism which rejects anything imperfect. It is the empty compensation, the deserving retribution for not being willing to love.

Battering infants because they wet the bed shows the same preference for fastidiousness over love as aborting babies because they might be deformed. Both are forms of spiritual suicide. The nightmare that torments the person who renounces love is the knowledge that he, because of his own imperfections, must be rejected as he once rejected others — for reasons of fastidiousness.

26

WHY HAVE A BABY, ANYWAY?

Population-control zealots,pro-abortionists, inflationary economists, and freedom philosophers have all occupied the public forum explaining in clear and simple rhetoric the many and compelling reasons that people should not desire children. The effect produced by these apostles of reason has been a set of nagging anxieties that have led straight to doubt and indecision about matters of conception, pregnancy, and birth. Fears of contributing to the population explosion, of carrying to term a less than normal baby, of not adequately providing for all the child's future economic needs, of being tied to an endless round of menial domestic chores, have mounted to a deafening crescendo leaving in the background one faint but nettling question: "Why have a baby, anyway?"

In the present age this is not an easy question to answer. Yet, surely there must be viable and acceptable reasons for having a baby, in spite of today's extraordinary adversity. A cursory examination of how this question was formerly answered may prove helpful.

In former years, according to the expressed popular opinion of the time, the reasons that parents wanted to have children fell neatly into six categories. These reasons varied from those which were private, marital, or familial, to those which were competitive, social, or philanthropic.

1) **Private:** A common reason for having a baby was to establish one's potency or demonstrate one's fertility. An equally common reason in this category could be found where women had been made insecure by the Freudian contention that their biological inferiority could be compensated only through pregnancy and maternity.

2) **Marital:** Another reason for having a baby was to plug a hole in an empty husband and wife relationship. Someone expressed it thus: "When I was 'it', and lived within my Mom, people said 'it' will be good for your marriage."

3) **Familial:** To continue the family name has been a time-honored reason for having a child. Those who have watched the King Henry VIII dramas on the motion picture screen or on TV have been forcefully convinced of how important it is to a father that he have a son to whom he can bequeath name, title, and wealth.

4) **Competitive:** Nothing used to be of greater comfort to parents of advanced middle age than knowing their children had not only succeeded but had done so on a grander scale than any of their friends' children.

5) **Social:** A noble and unselfish reason for having children was to help provide society with employable personnel. Socially responsible parents, mindful of someday having to withdraw from their socio-economic structure, used to arrange for their own replacement by having offspring.

6) **Philanthropic:** The loftiest motive for wanting children was the desire to continue the human race. This was the purest, most altruistic reason for wanting children and was found only in exceptional cases.

Such weak and shallow reasons for having children were not capable of withstanding the pressures coming from today's secular imperatives. The hole in each of these reasons is the omission of the value of the child. In each of the above categories, the child is viewed not as an independent, autonomous value but as either an extension of his parents or a servant of society.

Bertrand Russell became convinced that love for one's children must be a hoax when he noticed how quickly parents could overcome bereavement for their sons killed in combat to boast of that loss as a parental sacrifice to God and country. Love is not love which fails to recognize the other as other. One who is regarded as an extension ('chip off the old block') is not loved precisely as other. Nor is one loved who is regarded as merely filling a void ('we couldn't do without him'), or serving a social function ('cog in the machine'). Love requires the generosity of seeing the beloved in his own terms.

People want to have children for two fundamentally different reasons: 1) because there is something missing in their lives; 2) because of a super-abundance in their lives. The need of a sick person for a doctor is the opposite of the doctor's need to heal his patient. The former needs to receive, the latter needs to give. The need of the first originates from a lack in the patient (his bodily deficiencies); that of the second from a real possession in the doctor (his skill as a healer).

Wanting children merely because of a desire to fill a void is based on a lack and is selfish. On the other hand, wanting children because of a desire to give from one's substance is based on a real possession and is generous. It is only through generosity that love is possible because it is only through generosity that the other can be fully thematic, that is, the central and unselfish object of one's desire to give.

Plato states in his *Symposium* that happiness desires to express itself by reproducing the beautiful, either physically or spiritually. Love, too, desires by its own vital weight to repeat, share, or reproduce itself. Happiness and love exclude envy. They desire to celebrate what they are by making it happen again in a way that others can share. Through the generosity of love, every happiness desires that its own encore resound in the heart of another.

It should be quite natural, then, for a happy, loving married couple to desire to express that happiness by reproducing the beautiful — that is, by having children. People should not invent reasons for having children. For each reason they invent, some anti-natalist will invent an equally persuasive reason to the contrary. They should have children not for reasons but out of the super-abundant generosity of their being.

The present cultural confusion concerning why parents should want to have children may very well be symptomatic of a lack of marital happiness, love, and generosity. This is not to minimize or sidestep the practical exigencies which may at times make it imprudent to have children. It is to emphasize the point that the great things in life are not inspired by reasons that can be proclaimed from a public forum but by love which is intimately shared with another.

Anyone can understand the difficulties involved in having children. But if difficulty alone were reason for childlessness, then it would have also been reason for man's extinction.

27

THE PLAYBOY AND HIS MECHANICAL BRIDE: THE STERILE COUPLE

A cartoon in the *New Yorker* depicts a salesgirl recommending a certain brand of perfume to a young woman. "It smells like a new sport-car," she claims. The cartoon incisively points to what Marshall McLuhan has captioned in the title of his book *The Mechanical Bride*. The girl who competes successfully for the attention of the machine-minded male in a world of super-industrialization is precisely the one who has assumed the air of a machine. The Mechanical Bride is both the machine espoused by the industrial male and the girl who emulates the machine in order to win male attention and approval. Of course, "Mechanical Bride" also symbolizes a hopeless contradiction. A machine makes as loveless a bride as a bride makes an inefficient machine. Nonetheless, the modern male product of technology, the "Playboy", remains steadfast and undaunted in his unrelenting pursuit of her.

The same kind of artificial contradiction appears in the expression "vital statistics". Vitality, being a quality, cannot be numbered. Statistics, being based on quantity, cannot be animated. Life cannot be squeezed out of a number, nor can number be a life substitute. The "vital statistic" curve "36-24-36" represents the person as impersonal, and the body as abstract. Personality is always a distinguishing human characteristic. Numerability is the characteristic of a class of things. The woman whose essential attractiveness is presented in terms of a common statistic she shares with any number of other women suffers a suppression of her personality. Leslie Farber's remark that in the Playboy philosophy the fig leaf is removed from the genitals and placed over the face well expresses this preference for treating people as numbers rather than discovering them as unique persons.

The essential appeal numerating people rather than knowing them has its relative ease and convenience. "To place a person in a system," writes Abraham Maslow, "takes less energy than to know him in his own right, since in the former instance, all that has to be perceived is that one abstracted characteristic which indicates his belongingness in a class." It is simply easier for the young man who may be apprehensive about meeting and relating to a real woman, to be introduced to a glamorized photograph whose caption reassuringly enumerates the fact that this vicarious woman is acceptable because she possesses the proper and approved "vital statistics".

Similarly, the great and complex problems which confront mankind can be simplified by reducing them to a number. Zero-population-growth zealots think that achieving global solutions through limiting the people in the world to the 'right number' is a genuine insight. In actuality the zero-populationists are merely offering the latest convenient way of sidetracking attention from the real difficulties by emphasizing the most superficial aspect of human beings — their countability.

One of the popular justifications for abortion-on-request is the zero-population-growth philosophy. Eliminating a segment of the unborn will improve the chances of limiting the over-all population to a zero growth rate. This is just basic arithmetic. But it is exactly what is wrong with population numerologists. Basic arithmetic is not basic human decency. The elimination of any group of people will tend to hold down the over-all population figures. An adult is just as countable as a foetus when it comes to population arithmetic. To regard the unborn as simply a number that swells the population number is just a convenient way of ignoring their reality. It is a continuation of a mentality in which human beings are reduced to a set of statistical abstractions so that they do not have to be treated as distinct and substantial human beings who have rights and personalities of their own. The "Playboy" is the male who can't accept the woman. Abortion is the woman who can't accept the child. The woman is replaced by the 'hot number' with the approved "vital statistics". The aborted child is replaced with a numerical drop in the birth rate.

Sacrificing the unborn on the altar of a numerical ideal is choosing illusion over reality. Illusions in their pure, abstract, numerical, impersonal form can enslave the mind because they seem, in that transcendent state, more perfect and more enticing than anything found in reality. But they are empty. Reality may be difficult but the illusory world of numerical ideals is hopeless.

In a society so dominated by technology it is not astonishing that the "Mechanical Bride" rejects her offspring. Machines are not supposed to reproduce. Neither is it surprising that the "Playboy" rejects the woman for the "Mechanical Bride". The appeal of the stylized, efficient, controllable number who makes a complementary accessory to the "Playboy's" mechanized life-style is virtually irresistible to him. Yet the reality of the "Playboy's" mating with the "Mechanical Bride" and producing offspring who are aborted for the sake of a numerical ideal is more chillingly inhuman than any fantasy ever created by the science-fiction writer.

28

SOCIETY
AS AN
ART FORM

A Toronto newspaper has reported that some Canadian hospital committees have been approving the aborting of female babies believed carriers of the gene for muscular dystrophy. These babies themselves are unaffected by the gene. They may be perfectly healthy in all other respects and capable of living full and useful lives. But law allows that single sub-microscopic stain in their genetic code to be their fatal flaw, annulling all the blessings and joys to which these unborn babes are naturally heir.

The reason cited for aborting on these grounds was to prevent the gene for muscular dystrophy from being passed on to male offspring, who would then stand to suffer the ill-effect of the disease. Females are the ordinary carriers because infected males either do not live long enough (rarely beyond age twenty), or are not healthy enough to father children.

Some members of hospital committees consider abortion for such reasons to be a valid and effective approach to the muscular dystrophy problem now that the sex of the unborn can be determined with fair accuracy. Having the technical equipment, medical sanction, legal protection, and academic rationalizations to kill the unborn, scientists are now exploring submicroscopic horizons to discover new reasons for doing so.

A child can be aborted because it is probably female and possibly a carrier of the gene for muscular dystrophy. Even if the child *is* a female carrier, she may never have children. Furthermore, should the carrier have children, she might not have any males. If she does have males, they may be normal. If they are affected, they may still live normal lives, since it is quite possible that a cure for the disease may be discovered by that time.

Accepting abortions for such tenuous and hypothetical reasons is analogous to blowing up a passenger plane because a dangerous criminal might be aboard. What can be the motive for such overkill? Has society judged it better to destroy a healthy female carrier of a defective gene than to allow her to live and possibly infect a male? Does an unborn female have to justify her continued existence by the biological promise that she will never taint a male? Why hasn't "Women's Liberation" raised its voice against such sexist prejudice? Has society developed a morbid fear of the future? Have people lost faith in science's ability to cure diseases? Is kill better than cure? Is human procreation being more and more regarded as machine work whose products need better quality control?

Perhaps all these reasons play a part in the overkill syndrome. But more significantly, the central motivation may be the godless hope of generating a race of "beautiful people" to inhabit a "paradise" on earth. This is the desire for a society as an "art form" wherein each segment of the social fabric is created and controlled by the artists in power. The ideology behind the art-form society is taken from Machiavelli, and its implementation is secured through consolidating the power of the ruling class.

Machiavelli, a 16th century social philosopher, believed man to be a natural monstrosity. He taught that the use of force and compulsion was necessary in order to socialize the incorrigible masses. Machiavelli rejected the moral optimism of Christianity as impractical and unrealistic. As a "realist", he presumed that a stable society could not be maintained without recourse to actions which Christianity condemned. Morality, for Machiavelli, was expediency. It had nothing to do with natural law or God, with personal or transcendent values. Morality was what produced a good society — society taken as a work of art. Machiavelli is the first thoroughly modern thinker, because he prescinds from any considerations greater than society, such as God or goodness, and from any considerations smaller than society, such as the person or the group.

Society as an art-form is sculptured out of the unrefined mass of humanity which comprises the social artist's raw material. If only the end product of society, the resplendent art-form is recognized as a value, the defective, the unpromising, the recalcitrant, and the uncooperative may be remorselessly chipped away. Individuals who do not contribute to the "beautiful society" lose their justification for being, and may be removed from society as perfunctorily as stone shavings are swept from a sculptor's floor.

In order to maintain control of the art-form society, the power elite must ingratiate the masses by convincing them that they are controlling their own destiny. The power elite of politicians, doctors, lawyers, intellectuals, academicians, and military leaders controls people's lives while keeping them oblivious to that fact.

Women believe that abortion, contraception, and sterilization give them greater control of their bodies. In point of fact, it is the power elite that is controlling women's bodies, using technology as an intermediary. The power elite views abortion, contraception, and sterilization, which are power techniques to weed out undesirables, as its way of providing benefits for the society *it* controls.

The art-form society is the exact opposite of a free society. Dostoevsky saw this "prosperous social ant heap" as an example of compulsory goodness, rationalized mechanization, and enslaving necessity. He saw its designers as possessors of Euclidean minds operating in a spiritless world of three-dimensional space.

There can be no genuine life, no true development of personality, in the art-form society, because the self is not recognized as a value. And it is only the self who suffers and rejoices, lives and reflects. The art-form society is not a self; no feeling ever registers upon the antiseptic walls of its towering edifices or resounds within the automated hearts of its soul-less functionaries.

When a prominent Toronto geneticist was asked her views on aborting healthy females believed carriers of the gene for muscular dystrophy, she replied that she took "no personal stand" in such cases. And could she? It requires personality to take a personal stand on such issues. Slowly but methodically the art-form society seeks to rid itself of the human personality and the moral values by which that human personality thrives. Once personality has been cleared away, the path is open to the selective destruction of life for the purpose of producing a society of beautiful pawns.

The advocates of the art-form society harbor the deepest contempt for mankind. For them, natural man is personally unregenerate and can achieve a meaningful life only if he has first been depersonalized and artificially remade to fit an artistically designed social mold. This attitude represents pessimism in its most virulent form.

Italian scholars have shown that the difference between Dante and Machiavelli is that Dante could believe in both Heaven and Hell, whereas Machiavelli could believe only in Hell. It may very well be that pursuing their inhuman art-form society, pro-abortionists are preparing their own Hell. One can create only that in which he has faith.

29

THE NEW TEN COMMANDMENTS AND ABORTION

Privacy, point of view, specialization, financial independence, success, tolerance, career, mobility, technique and freedom: These are the holy icons which are pursued by today's man of the world with the kind of dedication which, by contrast, makes yesterday's man of God appear irresolute. They are the ten cultural commandments which contemporary society accepts unquestioningly and keeps religiously.

The basis for these cherished credos, although it escapes modern man's scrutiny, is a series of separations which isolate the individual from community participation.

1) **Privacy:** Privacy results from separating the individual from the group in space. Like modern Greta Garbos who "need to be alone", the man who is culturally "with it" is prepared to pay exorbitant prices for his geographical segregation from the rest of the populace. The urbanite must retreat to a private suburban residence to escape the discomfort of having to live with the results of his own mistakes. Locks, fences, walls, security guards, watch dogs, solitude, and seclusion are some of the high-priced items which symbolize modern man's need for privacy. The Sartrean maxim that "Hell is other people" achieves its cultural realization in today's social scrambling for privacy.

2) **Point of View:** Point of view results from separating the individual from the group with respect to thought. Today everyone is entitled to his own opinion on anything, and anyone who tries to impose his views on another is guilty of an unpardonable sin. In this atmosphere, education becomes nearly impossible and is often replaced by data accumulating, job training, social climbing, or supercilious pedantry. The pursuit of knowledge is fragmented by a kind of division of labor into 'rap sessions', panel discussions, and an endless number of meetings where private viewpoints are exchanged.

3) **Specialization:** Specialization results when the individual is separated from the group in work. The assembly-line

servant is virtually incapable of seeing the ethical connection between his narrow function and the use of the final product which his corporation produces. In higher education, the quest for new and original dissertation topics in increasingly specialized areas threatens to end any genuine communication between faculty members. Specialization has fragmented society to such a degree that society, as such, has begun to disappear, giving way to an agglomeration of diverse units which operate unaware of a relationship to any ultimate social purpose.

4) **Financial Independence:** Financial independence results when the individual is separated from the group with regard to economic dependence. The man who has 'arrived' no longer has to remain connected with society through employment in order to maintain his life style. He is an economic satellite unto himself who can do as he pleases. He can afford the luxury of contributing nothing to society, and feels no compelling reason to assist the economic needs of those who remain financially dependent. Full-time unemployment becomes his life ambition. Just as "money is the poor man's credit card," employment is the poor man's occupation.

5) **Success:** Success results, according to its peculiar cultural interpretation, when the individual is separated from the group with regard to status. Star status symbolizes not only distance from others but distance above others. To find 'room at the top' where one can lord above others is the driving ambition of anyone who wants to be a success. To be stationed conspicuously on top of the social world is success's truest emblem. No one succeeds in obscurity. The greater the success, the higher the status and the wider the separation from the common man.

6) **Tolerance:** Tolerance, in its new and non-Christian sense, results when the individual is separated from the group with regard to his moral responsibility to it. With each person "doing his own thing," no one should second-guess the peculiar behavior patterns of others. "Live and let live" becomes the motto of the man of tolerance who "judges not, lest he be judged." *Laissez-faire* existentialism signifies a policy of mutual non-interference in all moral matters. Such tolerance makes a soft pillow for a divorce lawyer's conscience.

7) Career results when work is separated from domesticity, or the family group. The farmer never had a career because his work was too closely bound up with his household. When man's work has nothing to do with his home, he then has a career. The modern cult of gracious living requires that the living room be swept clear of any signs of toil. The ironing board and vacuum cleaner must be kept hidden from the eye of a guest. The career man comes home to rest or entertain but not to work. In this way, the career man becomes a visitor or even a stranger in his own home, as Dagwood is a bum in his

own homestead.

8) **Mobility:** Mobility results when man is separated from his roots, or ancestral group. The "man on the move", the "go-getter", the "social climber", and the "status seeker" must be highly mobile in order to improve their chances for success. The extended family gives way to the streamlined nuclear family to facilitate family mobility in moving from job to job, and from opportunity to opportunity. Lateral mobility via cars, trains, and planes becomes a standardized prerequisite for vertical upward mobility.

9) **Technique:** Technique, as its own value, results when means is separated from end. Without a clear, overriding purpose for society, technique becomes its own purpose — an end unto itself. Scholars have pointed out that when man becomes blind to ends, he becomes obsessed with means. When means are no longer tempered and proportioned to serve higher ends, they become objects of fanatical devotion. The essence of fanaticism is precisely the obsession with the part resulting from obliviousness to the whole. This leads to the fallacy of technologism — that because a thing can be done, it must be done. The technological possible becomes identified with the moral imperative.

10) **Freedom:** Freedom, in the present cultural sense, results from separating act from responsibility. "Let the chips fall where they may" symbolizes the thirst for activity unaccompanied by reflection. If an act is tied to a responsibility, then it is not free. Acts are pure and free only when they are severed from a concern for their consequences. The freedom of an act flows from a personal free choice against which no law or group of moralists should inveigh. Freedom belongs to an individual as a natural right and should never be constrained by external forces.

* * * * * * * * *

The recent wave of tolerance to abortion-on-demand and abortion-on-virtual-demand is consistent with the new ten cultural commandments modern society has taken to its heart.

1) The January 22, 1973, United States Supreme Court decision on abortion upheld a woman's right to abort her child on the basis that her right to *privacy* takes precedence over her child's right to live. The unborn child, although biologically and individually distinct from the mother, can be legally expropriated by her. Considered as part of his mother's body, the unborn falls not under the protection of law but under the dominion of will. Unwanted pregnancies are viewed as invasions

of privacy. Abortions are recognized as exercising one's constitutional right. Thus, in the eyes of the United States Supreme Court no human being can come into existence without potentially violating someone's right to privacy.

2) One of the most commonly heard defenses of elective abortion, even from those who may be privately opposed to abortion, is that each person has a right to his own *point of view,* and that no one should impose his moral viewpoint on another. No doubt this fact gives rise to the impression that more people approve of abortion than actually do. In a society where moral isolation is a high cultural value, people shy away from even thinking that the emperor may be naked.

3) One often hears that abortion is merely a medical matter between the pregnant mother and her doctor. This is the myopia of *specialization.* The foetus is not an individual, a human, a self, a value, or a life. He is the object of a specialist's practice. He is nothing more than something an abortion specialist can abort. Justice never enters the picture. The abortion specialist approaches his foetal object with knowledge, skill, and moral blinders.

The argument "since abortion is a *private* matter between the pregnant woman and her *specialist* doctor, no one else should try to impose his *point of view* on her," is a kind of oath of allegiance to the first three cultural commandments. Although aware of the origin of these credos, the pro-abortionist swears his fidelity to them in this form of pseudo-argumentation.

4) Rearing a child is an obvious expense. If one's concern for *financial independence,* whether of a partial or complete sort, is greater than his regard for the unborn child, then abortion becomes justifiable. The government, rather than offer assistance to indigent families who may want the child but not the financial burden he would impose, paves the way for easier abortions for socio-economic reasons. Some families can not afford children and the government does not believe it can not afford to kill them. Money becomes more valuable than life, and financial independence becomes more holy than justice.

5) Stern, an internationally popular magazine published in 1971 the signatures of 374 movie actresses, celebrities, and others who confessed having undergone illegal abortions. This publication followed a similar collection of "public confessions" supplied by 343 French women in April of the same year. The unwanted child, when he gets in the way of *success,* becomes expendable. Babies are aborted not only for reasons of indigence but for reasons of success. These shameless public declarations of abortions identify success with loss of moral sensitivity as if "glamorhood" superseded motherhood.

6) Today's open-minded, liberated citizen is a model of *tolerance.* In a pluralistic society, where people's tastes, preferences, and moral sensibilities differ radically, the modern man takes a tolerant view of abortion. Like Pontius Pilate before him, he washes his hands of issues that require moral insight and personal courage. Everyone becomes his own moral philosopher, and slowly society loses the very consensus of moral purpose which is necessary to keep it human.

7) Today's woman, envious of her husband's *career,* which carries him to exotic lands and places outside the home, is impatient to follow him. The thought of unwanted pregnancies and unwanted children that incarcerate her in the home oppresses her. She must have a career, and that means emancipation from the house and from unwanted children. Abortion symbolizes this new freedom from the demeaning status of domestic servant and heralds for many the entrance to a new and exciting career life. But maybe there's a hitch. "Why would a woman want to be the same thing to everyone when she can be everything to someone?" Chesterton's disturbing question is not raised very often, for it is incompatible with the policy of never questioning basic cultural values.

8) Children, as Alvin Toffler states in *Future Shock,* are regarded as "clutter" to the streamlined nuclear family on the move. Upward *mobility* requires trimming a family to the bare essentials. Changing jobs and locations and travelling to conventions and vacation spots necessitate minimizing the number of people in the family. Untimely pregnancies that interfere with the rhythm of one's social climbing are to be terminated. Babies have a place in the world, but their time of arrival must harmonize with a rather strict and uncompromising social calendar.

9) Abortion, says one obstetrician, is a good "armamentarium" for the doctor to have at his disposal. The word "armamentarium" in Latin means "arsenal". The Medical profession has the *technique* and the technology; why not put them into practice? Aborting because the equipment and methodology are available is the urbane equivalent of the frontiersman's mentality, "Have gun will travel." Technically, abortion seems so easy a procedure, especially in the early weeks of pregnancy, that the temptation to employ it can be very difficult to resist. As Henrik Ibsen has pointed out, when a pistol is seen hanging on the wall in the first act, the audience can conclude its use before the play is over. Once man divorces technique from purposes, he does things simply because they can be done. When Louis Untermeyer, in the final line of his poem "Portrait of a Machine," concisely describes man as "the slave to what his slaves create," he is referring to the power technology can have over man. Man can become the victim as well as the exe-

cutioner when he does not employ his technology in the service of human values.

10) Disengaging act from responsibility to produce pure freedom disposes one to a continuously repeating pattern of disengagements. Such freedom requires that meaning be dissociated from sex, sex from conception, conception from delivery, and delivery from rearing. It logically implies that abortion be removed from the criminal code or simply from law altogether. Pure freedom becomes an absolute value. It is an unconditioned, unqualified good. As is the case with atheistic existentialism, it is not so much what is chosen that counts, but that it was chosen freely. Pro-abortionist women demand they be given the freedom to determine whether or not they should continue a pregnancy. The freedom to abort is accepted as a more basic human value than the responsibility to care.

* * * * * * * * *

All of these ten cultural commandments which give rise to the commonly repeated arguments for abortion-on-request are based on a division which separates and isolates the individual from the group and from his responsibilities toward members of that group. It is not merely coincidental that abortion itself represents a separation. It is the final and most intimately personal separation of a mother from her own child.

Pro-abortionist arguments are logically mounted on a premise that denies community, integration, love, care, and justice. Although they present themselves as liberated and sophisticated, in truth, because they are ignorant of their own first premises, pro-abortionists are serfs to culture and slaves to fashion. Abortion is the final symptom of a society which has lost its sense of community. At an hour when society, if it is to be preserved, needs the most human and generous responses from its members, the abortion mentality represents an accelerating movement towards its collapse.

It has been observed that people run faster the more they fear they are lost. The drowning man stiffens at the moment his life depends on how well he is able to relax. When a man is afire, running serves only to fan the flames. These images capture the state of panic which the abortionist mind represents. If there is to be any reversal of this state, it will take place only when people take a more detached view of their cultural credos. By examining the unnatural foundations for today's "New Ten Commandments" and studying their adoption's dehumanizing effect, man may realize the vanity of fleeing from his own humanity and being to construct a society based on integrating the values that accord with human personality.

Man will not achieve a more human society without practising a more spiritual religion; for religion is society's bedrock basis. Arnold Toynbee has trenchantly characterized the present idolatrous religion of private wealth as follows:

> Our present religion is a consecration of egoism. Our present ultimate objective is the anti-social pursuit of material gain, both individual and collective.

With such a divisive religion can it be at all surprising that modern man has made himself so lonely and so miserable?

—30—
DIARY OF AN EXPECTANT MOTHER

W I can't wait until this pregnancy is over with.
H I can't wait until he sleeps through the night.
E I can't wait until he's out of diapers.
N I can't wait until he starts talking.
  I can't wait until he can feed himself.
A I can't wait until he starts school.
R
E   When is he going to listen to me?
      When is he going to start showing his parents some
Y   respect?
O   When is he going to start cleaning up his room?
U   When is he going to start giving me some help around
         this place?
G   When is he going to overcome his shyness with girls?
O
I I'll be glad when he gets a part time job.
N I'll be glad when he decides what college he'll go to.
G I'll be glad when he makes up his mind about what career
  he wants.
T I'll be glad when he finally gets established in his
O   profession.
  I'll be glad when he settles down and gets married.
G
R   I can't wait until the wedding plans are finalized.
O   I can't wait until I see them in their new apartment.
W   I can't wait until they get out of that crummy
         apartment.
U   I can't wait until I see my new grandchild.
P   I can't wait until they go on vacation and leave my
?   grandson with me so we can really get to know
         each other.

I picked up the extension the other day, Ethel. I wasn't eavesdropping mind you. I didn't know my darling son was on the other line. Do you know what that thankless good-for-nothing said? "I can't wait until I get Mom into a home." After all I've done for him.

Ethel: Children never appreciate what you do for them. It's a rotten shame.

VI

A STRATEGY IN REVIEW

"The world is still
deceived with
ornament.
In law, what plea so
tainted and
corrupt,
But, being season'd
with a gracious
voice,
Obscures the show
of evil? In
religion,
What damned error,
but some sober
brow
Will bless it, and
approve it with a
text,
Hiding the gross-
ness with fair
ornament?
There is no vice so
simple, but
assumes
Some mark of
virtue on his out-
ward parts:
How many cowards,
whose hearts are
all as false
As stairs of sand,
wear yet upon
their chins
The beards of Her-
cules and frown-
ing Mars;
Who, inward
search'd, have
livers white as
milk;
And these assume
but valour's
excrement
To render them
redoubted!" — Shakespeare

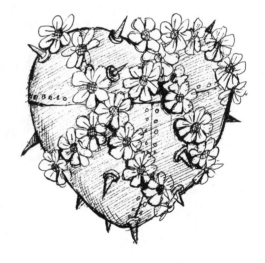

PARALLELS
IN
TREACHERY

Plutarch's *Lives,* an ancient biographical account of famous Greeks and Romans, supplied the basic source material for Shakespeare's *Julius Caesar* and Dante's treatment of Brutus and Cassius in his *Divine Comedy.* Each of these literary dramas dealt with the crimes of betrayal and murder which Brutus, Cassius, and their fellow conspirators perpetrated against their master, Julius Caesar. In Shakespeare, the dramatic re-enactment of these crimes is central to the play. In Dante, the form of punishment Brutus and Cassius warrant, although incidental to the poem as a whole, is nonetheless a focal point in the final canto of the "Inferno". Shakespeare portrays the human crime; Dante, the divine punishment.

In our own time, the abortionists' plot to kill the unborn bears a striking resemblance in style, development, and logic to the Romans' conspiratorial plan to kill Caesar. The parallels of treachery between the two can be revealed with considerable diversity and detail by using selected texts from *Julius Caesar* and comparing them with correlative incidents from the present record of the abortionists' propaganda.

Six major stages in the development of the plot to kill Caesar are comparable to the abortionists' plot to kill the unborn. Crime, no matter how monstrous, can be rationalistically justified if the conspirators possess sufficient patience and serpentine cunning. Following this treatment, the improbable human conjunction of murder and "noblest Roman of them all" is discussed. In the concluding part is offered some reflections concerning the appropriateness, in the mind of Dante, of regarding the crimes of Brutus and Cassius with such pitiless contempt.

Rarely does a faction conceive, design, and execute a murder without accompanying it with a string of rationalizations which offer to prove not only the justification of the crime but even its moral excellence. The conspirators led by Marcus Brutus and Gaius Cassius do precisely this. Armed with rhetoric, deceits, and oratory, they argue the righteousness of their plot to kill Caesar, setting out the stages for such successful argumentation accordingly:

1

PRESENT THE VICTIM IN THE IMAGE OF A WORTH-LESS ENTITY

Since, in conscience, it is much easier to kill a snake than to kill a Caesar, Brutus engages in this particular form of dehumanizing his master:

Think him as a serpent's egg
Which Hatch'd would as his kind grow mischievous,
And kill him in the shell. (II, 1, 32)

This is the facile transformation of the great Caesar, "The foremost man of all the world", to the status of a serpent's egg. Not only would crushing a serpent's egg not be a crime, but it would indeed be an act of meritorious significance.

The National Observer reported early in 1972 that the abortion of a nine-week foetus was being shown on film to thousands of college students in the United States. William Baird, a well known pro-abortionist, comforts the young woman who undergoes the abortion by describing the abortus (the removed foetus) to her as marmalade. He does not point out that an electroencephalograph can pick up the brain waves of even a six week human foetus. The nine-week foetus suffers the transmogrification from brain-active human being to *marmalade* or *pre-foetus!*

It is very common to hear the human embryo referred to as mere protoplasm, or a blob of tissue, or an unwanted part of the mother's viscera. Thorough dehumanization is the first step in the rationalistic methodology of murder.

2

DISARM THE OPPOSITION WITH SMILES AND AFFABILITY

When the conspirators convene, Brutus offers the following suggestion for effectively concealing from the eyes of the public the evil nature of their plot:

O conspiracy
Sham'st thou to show thy dang'rous brow by night,
When evils are most free? O, then by day
Where wilt thou find a cavern dark enough
To mask so monstrous visage: Seek none, conspiracy
Hide it in smiles and affability!
For if thou path, thy native semblence on,
Not Erebus itself were dim enough
To hide thee from prevention. (II, 1, 81)

In his account of the 1971 abortion symposium in Los Angeles, sociologist Paul Marx describes the conspirators present as "Death Peddlers". Marx reports that not only were smiles and affability the order of the day, but those in attendance regaled themselves in loud and recurrent laughter as if they needed a thicker mask to shield any suggestion of foul play. Dr. Irwin Kaiser spoke at one of the general sessions. As his contribution to the merrymaking, he commented that if abortionists were prepared to enter the competitive New York market where abortion fees ranged as high as $1,500 they'd make a substantial killing. His black levity was met with great laughter from the audience.

Members of the medical profession have been warned many times by pro-abortionists not to express discourtesy or assume a moralizing attitude to an abortion patient. Abortion itself is to be sloughed over, and a questioning countenance is strictly forbidden. Could an exterior of smiles and affability possibly house an inner spectre? Surely the devil never smiles!

(3)

CONVINCE THE ASSASSINS THEY ARE PRIESTLY LIBERATORS

Brutus, approximating a religious leader, reminds Cassius of the holy deed they are about to commit:

Let us be sacrificers, but not butchers, Gaius. (II, 1, 175)
Let's carve him as a dish fit for the gods. (II, 1, 182)
We shall be called purgers, not murderers. (II, 1, 189)

The word 'butcher' is commonly used by abortionists to refer to the illegal abortion practicioner who supposedly performs his sordid deed in a 'back alley'. How curiously the blessing of legality transforms butchers into priests! Abortionists see their work as humanitarian. Many claim to love the unborn too much to allow them to suffer lives of rejection outside the womb. A lawyer suggests that the unborn need advocates to argue for their death. A clergyman contends that the foetus needs someone to argue on behalf of his right not to be born.

These humanitarians sacrifice the unwanted unborn for a better quality of life and a more liberated society. Also, by some bizarre twist of logic, an aborted sacrificial lamb can bring its murderers close together. Obstetrician Robert E. Hall states that "Love may even be enriched by going through the experience of having an abortion together".

Abortionists see themselves as purgers. Through abortion things are made better; life is purified. The death of the foetus improves his lot. Possible rejection, disease, or deformity is, to these holy humanitarians, a fate worse than death. Given such lofty ideals as improving the quality of human life, how can such humanitarians ever be considered murderers?

(4)

CONVINCE THE ASSASSINS ONLY AN ABSTRACTION WILL BE LOST

Brutus, assuredly, holds no personal grudge against Caesar. In fact, he is not going to deal with Caesar at all. He will vanquish the spirit of Caesar, that ambition which is such a "grievous fault". This spirit, of course, is a mere abstraction, and one cannot murder an abstraction. If Caesar does bleed, it is an unfortunate, unintended, and incidental effect of slaying his spirit of ambition.

We all stand up against the spirit of Caesar
And in the spirit of men there is no blood.
O that we then could come by Caesar's spirit
And not dismember Caesar. But alas,
Caesar must bleed for it! (II, 1, 176)

The renowned philosopher-theologian Joseph Fletcher has asserted, "There is no such thing as embryonic human life nor a person being 'in utero'. It is a faith proposition that there is such a thing as an unborn baby".

Fletcher would have his colleagues believe that the foetus is an invisible wraith, a virtual abstraction permanently shielded from the hopeful eye of either the fetologist or the embryologist. Indeed, there is no such thing as the science of fetology or embryology!

What is it, then, which is destroyed in an abortion? Everyone sympathizes with the woman who is distressed by an unwanted pregnancy. Everyone stands up against a woman's being impregnated against her will. If only these regrettable impositions could be slain directly, there would be no blood. If the foetus must die, it is to be remembered that it was not because of what he was or anything he did but because of the untimely and unpleasant burden which attended him. Abortion cannot be murder, for what is directly killed is insubstantial and abstract.

(5)

GIVE CENTRAL PROMINENCE TO SOME HYPOTHETICAL GOOD WHICH MIGHT RESULT FROM THE CRIME

Cassius and Brutus seek to convince one another that not only are they doing Caesar a favour by killing him but they are actually his good friends for doing so. In sparing Caesar the fearful anguish of awaiting the unknown hour of his natural death, his assassins pay him a loving kindness. Friendship knows no bounds. Even murder can be a gesture of friendliness:

Cassius:	Why, he that cuts off twenty years of life Cuts off so many years of fearing death.
Brutus:	Grant that, and then death is a benefit So are we Caesar's friends, that have abridged His time of fearing death. (III, 1, 111)

The Reverend Hugh Anwyl contends that a counselor should assist a pregnant woman to determine "what for her would be the loving act in her particular situation". If the environment into which the child would be brought promised to be unfavourable for him, then abortion would be the "loving act". The friendly, loving act of abortion would avert a possible life of needless suffering for the child. Also, if the foetus were defective, then the decision to abort him could be considered loving. Hence, abortion confers a good, namely, deliverance from the causes which would produce a life of rejection, degradation, or misery.

All too commonly, abortionists argue that avoiding possible future misfortune for the mother or child is a good of such importance as to overshadow the minor misfortune of not being born. In that case we might all do well to commit suicide to avoid all possible future misfortune. The abortionists insist that preventing birth can be a good thing. And, after all, isn't one who does a good thing for another a friend?

(6)

PERSUADE THE POPULACE THAT THE CRIME WAS DESIGNED FOR THEIR BENEFIT
AND THAT THE RESULTS WILL SERVE ONLY THEIR GOOD

Brutus, Cassius, and the other conspirators, self-effacing noble Romans that they were, thought only of the good of their country. They saw themselves as "The men that gave their country liberty" (III, 1, 129). When Caesar was slain they cried, "Peace, freedom and liberty!" (III, 1, 120). Shortly thereafter they reinforced their cry with "Liberty, freedom, enfranchisement" (III, 1, 188). They were trained rhetoricians and adroit sloganeers. Their simplicity and directness, combined with the efficiency and ease with which they spoke, reassured the populace. Sincerity, patriotism, and the desire for the public good aptly characterized the conspirators.

Cries of "Liberty and Freedom" are perhaps the most frequently used rhetorical devices of libertarian abortionists. Dr. Robert Hall envisions the wedding of *Sexual Freedom* and a national *Liberal Abortion Law* as the introduction of a "Golden Age". The sexual problem is solved by merely making it "free" to the public, i.e., without any legal or moral disapprobation. The unwanted pregnancy problem is solved by merely making abortion laws "liberal", thereby giving every woman the right to choose. Simply conjoining sex with freedom, and abortion with liberty, brings about a national cure for a national crisis. There is true magic in rhetoric and slogans. The populace will hear only what it is willing to hear; the dream of a golden age is too tempting to pass up. Tell people what they want to hear and give them what they want to have, and they'll be happy.

The Roman conspirators, in the words of Mark Van Doren, "All have something of the statue in them". They stand tall, their vision taken from a lofty eminence. They exist only for Rome and the hope of a brighter future. In this regard they are truly noble. But like statues, they are without selves and consequently cannot make a gift of themselves to their immediate loved ones. They dwell aloofly in a realm of distant dreams and thin abstractions. They speak uniformly, as if trained in a common forensic academy. Where reason threatens their vision, they sacrifice it for rhetoric. When intuition of woman calls them to earth, their noble stratagems summon them away again.

Much of the same is true of the abortionists. Their view is beyond the humble foetus. They see crowded worlds and burdened women, urban jungles and impoverished nations. At the prospect of unredeemable pain their heart falters. At the portent of invincible discord their hope sinks. Their struggle is with the abstractions of death and despair. Their goal is a future which bears little resemblance to the present. The living foetus utters his pathetic plea but cannot be heard, because he lies in the way of the "Golden Age".

The abortionists do not accept that there can be no earthly utopias. They do not reckon that life must consist in loving those who are nearest. The nearest of any two lives are the mother and her unborn child. If love and care do not take root here, everything that is promised man is a baseless and empty fiction. If we loved only those we could embrace, we would not need the noble mien that seeks the global paradise. The abortionists, in sacrificing everything on an immediate personal level for a golden future, lose the future too. Where can there be hope in a world in which the epitaph for the unborn is *"Et Tu Mater!"*

* * * * * * * *

The farfetched and desperate attempts of both the conspirators and the abortionists to whitewash their crimes reveal the deeply personal penalty they must pay for such rank and thoroughgoing dishonesty. The total inobjectivity, self-delusion, irrationality, and moral blindness exemplified by these criminals require that the penalty be paid in a deterioration of the very faculties which they had prostituted to make the crimes appear justifiable. This deterioration appears to be so advanced in the case of the conspirators and the abortionists as to amount to the virtual death of their spirituality. This is precisely their punishment. To commit such acts of moral treachery is to punish oneself by the erosion and diminishment of one's soul. Hence the inseparability of crime and punishment. Punishment can no more be separated from crime than death can be separated from suicide, or loneliness from fratricide.

As Shakespeare's play has served to dramatize the crimes of Brutus and Cassius, Dante's poem may now be enlisted to describe their punishment.

In the *Inferno,* Dante proportions the suffering of the condemned to the nature and gravity of their earthly sins. He places the three who are to suffer most in the centre of Hell's ninth circle, each of them ripped and raked by the teeth of Satan himself. In a grotesque parody of the Trinity, Dante portrays Satan as three-headed. Eternally clamped and torn in his central mouth is Judas Iscariot. In his mouths on either side, enduring similar but less severe eternal torments, are Marcus Brutus and Gaius Cassius.

"That soul that suffers most," explained my guide
"is Judas Iscariot, he who kicks his legs
on the fiery chin and has his head inside.

Of the other two, who have their heads thrust
    forward,
the one who dangles down from the black face
is Brutus: note how he writhes without a word.

And there, with the huge and sinewy arms, is the soul
of Cassius." (Canto XXXIV, 61)

Why, in Dante's view, do Brutus, "the noblest Roman of them all", and his honourable compatriot deserve such extreme infernal punishment? Like Judas, both Brutus and Cassius were guilty of "treachery against their master" and soon thereafter committed suicide. But perhaps there was something else in their approach to life and death which would illumine the nature of their treachery:

The thirty shekels Judas received promised to secure for him a sunny day in the future. Unfortunately that day never came. To Brutus and Cassius, the murder of Caesar promised a future of peace, liberty, and freedom. That day did not arrive. "He who fights the future", wrote Kierkegaard, "has a dangerous enemy". The future is not; it is an abstraction. The present is all man has. In the words of Judas's victim, "the evil of the day is sufficient thereof". It may be noble and honourable to sacrifice the present self for the future dream. Indeed, Brutus and Cassius were noble and honourable men. But to disregard the immediate friend, the burning love, the present trust, for what is not, is simply to shun life itself. One can be numbed by nobility. Then the only life he has, that which saturates his hour at hand, is exchanged for abstract nothingness. There is profound ingratitude in this stance. It is perhaps in consequence of this sin that the most profound pain is deserved. The now is not perfect, but it is all one ever has. It is the man — not the plan — who enriches and enlightens each successive day. The future gets its substance from man's present love, not his calculated plan.

Brutus and Cassius detest life and bargain for an impossible earthly vision. Caesar stands in the way. So he must be slain. The abortionists detest life, with its grim compromises with intolerable imperfection. The foetus lies in the way. So he must be aborted. To accept the present with all its imperfections, to receive friends with all their limitations, takes more than reason. It takes greatness. It takes love. The perfect life requires nothing of man. What the abortionists cannot understand is that humanitarians must first be human. To be human is to rejoice in one's littleness and to illumine each tomorrow through the greatness of love, the patience of hope, and the power of faith.

In Dante, Brutus writhes in eternal wordlessness, an appropriate punishment for the man whose words of rationalistic counsel poisoned his conspirators. In Shakespeare, Brutus early prophesies:

Between the acting of a dreadful thing
and the first motion, all the interim is
like a phantasma or a hideous dream.
The genius and the mortal instruments
are then in council. (II, 1, 63)

It is fitting, for Dante, that the mouth of the devil be the source of torture for the three whose act of betrayal came from their own mouths.

Cassius, who "hears no music", "loves no plays", and "seldom smiles" (I, 2, 210), is condemned to suffer the gloom of the inner circle, where his soul remains unheard, unloved, and unnoticed. He was distant from the pulse of earthly life. In death he remains distant, even from the pitiless gaze of the condemned.

It is most ironic that the Reverend Hugh Anwyl opened his address at the 1971 California Abortion Symposium by quoting from Dante's *Inferno,* glibly referring to hell as "that mythical place". The logic that represses the crime must also repress the punishment.

According to T. S. Eliot, "Dante and Shakespeare divided the world between them. There is not third". We might do well to listen to our literary masters.

—32—

PROPAGANDA, DIALOGUE, AND ABORTION

Almost everyone wants to participate in 'dialogue'. Whether in the form of 'rap session', 'panel discussion', 'encounter group', or 'ecumenical gathering', dialogue has taken its place alongside of Mom and apple pie as a sacrosanct and universal institution. On the other hand, no one seeks propaganda.

With so wide a popularity gulf separating dialogue from propaganda, one might think that no one could confuse them. Yet nothing could be further from the truth.

At the beginning of the Second World War, members of the British Intelligence discovered, to their amazement, that it was literally impossible to convince any member of the German army that he was the victim of Nazi propaganda. Hannah Arendt reported in her book *Eichmann in Jerusalem* that it was easy for Adolf Eichmann to remain convinced that exterminating the Jewish population was moral, because he had never met a colleague who completely opposed such an action.

The true victim of propaganda is so immersed in the narrowness of his views that he is unable to participate in dialogue. The whole point of propaganda is to get the victim to see propaganda, one finds a characteristic form which has recurred necting the word propaganda to the doctrines they spread.

History tells us two things about propaganda: 1) human beings are highly prone to fall victims to it; 2) having fallen to it, human beings are often unable to see their situation for what it is.

Considering the abortion controversy in this context, one may ask which side is involved in propaganda and which side is engaged in honest dialogue. The question is crucial.

Looking a little more deeply into the structure of propaganda, one finds a characteristic form which has recurred throughout history. This form involves an uncompromising striving for the realization of a single, clearly defined objective.

Contemporary man falls victim to various propaganda myths which are codified in the form of single-meaning words: "success"; "Money"; "Power"; "Progress"; "Gross-National-Product"; "Gracious-Living". In the motion picture *The Graduate,* Ben is given a single all-inclusive image upon which to structure his life — "Plastics". "Plastics" as a career goal constricts a person within a tight system, closed off from the possibility of dialogue. Thus, "Plastics" becomes propaganda.

Likewise, the "love" espoused by the "flower children", the "freedom" championed by *Women's Lib,* the "rights" endorsed by pro-abortionists, fall into propaganda structures. Each is characterized by single, clearly defined objectives which close off dialogue with their opposites.

Those involved in dialogue are suspicious of single-word panaceas. They talk of love *and* justice; freedom *and* responsibility; rights *and* duties. Love alone degenerates into sentimentality; harmonized with justice it has infinite potential. Freedom alone becomes either license or loneliness; allied with responsibility it gains a positive direction. Rights alone is empty legalism; united with duty, it becomes a living reciprocity of giving and receiving. Even with God, justice untempered by mercy is cruel; power without love, egoistic; love without forgiveness, proud.

Advocates of dialogue see life not as monolithic, but as multi-dimensional. The *One-Dimensional Man* has been propagandized. So too has the "company man", the "organization man". "Sexism" is propaganda whether it is the "sexism" of "J", or "M", or "M" and "J".[1] On the other hand, the authors of dialogue insist that truth cannot be squeezed into a single-meaning word. Consider Martin Buber's *I-Thou,* Paul Tillich's *Love, Justice and Power,* Dostoevsky's *Crime and Punishment,* Henri Bergson's *Time and Free-Will,* Martin Heidegger's *Being and Time,* Gabriel Marcel's *Being and Having,* Jacques Maritain's *The Person and the Common Good,* Haim Ginnott's *Between Parent and Child,* Bruno Bettelheim's *Love is not Enough,* and Rollo May's *Love and Will* and *Power and Innocence.* Like Aristotle, who taught that virtue was in the "mean" between two extremes, these authors of dialogue seek a reconciliation between opposites, a unity of diversity.

The propagandist becomes so beguiled by a single truth that he isolates it from the context which gave it life and value. Then, oblivious to everything else, he makes of his singularized truth an all-encompassing idol. In propagandizing this single element of truth, he loses dialogue with the rest of reality. Py-

[1]The pseudonymous authors of *The Sensuous Woman, The Sensuous Man;* and Masters and Johnson.

thagoras was so impressed with number that he could see nothing else. He became a propagandist when he sought to explain all reality in terms of number. Nazi Germany could see no truth other than the purity of the Aryan race. Spanish Inquisitors could see no value other than faith. Victorians could see no virtue other than civility. Narcissus could see no reality other than his own extended image.

When the pro-abortionist talks about freedom without responsibility, rights without duties, individualism without care, convenience without sacrifice, mother without child, quality of life without the right to life, love without justice, government without morality, and motherhood without fatherhood, then he or she is spouting pure propaganda.

—33—

AVOIDING UNWANTED PREGNANCIES AND ELIMINATING UNWANTED CHILDREN THROUGH THE MAGIC OF THE SLOGAN

"A bourgeois who has not lost his illusions is like a winged hippopotamus." — Leon Bloy

Life, at best, is down to earth. Progress is slow, work is tedious, horizons are limited, time is short, and death is inevitable. Perhaps this is why man cherishes illusions and believes in magic. They offer him a much desired antidote for the weightiness of life.

One of man's favorite illusions is his belief that slogans can realistically serve the cause of a moral revolution. By reducing reality to a placard, philosophy to a catch phrase, and thought to a conditioned reflex, the slogan provides the illusion of an easily manageable world in which all problems are curable.

One particular slogan, espoused by Planned Parenthood, is credited with having the key to solving the perennial problems of the unwanted pregnancy and the unwanted child. "Every child should be wanted and needed." In a slogan world of primal innocence and utopian simplicity this makes perfect sense. But in a world of harsh reality this slogan proves as uplifting to man as are wings to a hippopotamus.

The subjunctive mood ("should be") of the slogan does not take into account the distance that separates what should be from what actually is. In other words, the slogan does not reflect the real problems contained in improving the way things are so that they become more like the way things should be. The wings given to the hippopotamus lack the power to get him airborne. By the same token, the information contained in the slogan is insufficient to explain why, indeed, "So many unwanted pregnancies occur and so many unwanted children exist". The information which the slogan omits is precisely what needs to be known, namely, why there are unwanted pregnancies, and why there are unwanted babies.

Everyone agrees that both pregnancies and children should be wanted and needed. Everyone also agrees that abortion is an unpleasant experience. In order to put an end to unwanted pregnancies, unwanted children, and induced abortions, Planned Parenthood and others have devised the following strategy: "Every child should be wanted and needed." Thus, wanted pregnancies should be planned; unwanted pregnancies should be avoided. Therefore, with sound sex education programs in the schools, and easy access to effective contraceptives, all pregnancies will be planned and all children will be wanted. So the argument runs. It is clear and convincing enough to enlist the services of a good many hard-working humanitarians. However, there are three erroneous assumptions in its initial premise. These assumptions are precisely what must be examined if the distance of separation between the actual world of people and the ideal world symbolized by the slogan is fully to be appreciated. The assumptions are as follows:

1) Men and women are so consciously aware of the consequences of intercourse that pregnancies never result from subconscious motivations.

2) A woman either wants or does not want to become pregnant; her feelings in this regard are never ambivalent or inconsistent.

3) The reasons a woman may want or need a pregnancy (or conceive a child), whatever they may be, are necessarily legitimate ones.

Even a superficial inspection of the relevant data available in psychiatric and psychological literature is sufficient to disclose the illegitimacy of these assumptions.

1) Rollo May, author and psychotherapist, cites the case of a patient whose periodic impotence coincided with his wife's monthly fertile period. This temporary impotence occurred despite the fact that both he and his wife consciously wished to have a baby. It was learned, through consultation, that subcon-

sciously the husband did not want to father a child who would be a rival for his wife's affection, but preferred to remain himself as her baby.[1]

From Freud to the present, thousands of case histories have been recorded which offer testimony to the significant role the subconscious can play in influencing decisions to choose, reject, or avoid pregnancy. Even in the healthiest, most consciously motivated lives, attitudes to so profound and mysterious a phenomenon as sex and reproduction are bound to contain some element of subconscious influence. The deep and transcendent implications of procreation, which links man to the creative pulse of the cosmos and unites him to the future generations of his race, cannot be brought completely under conscious control. Attitudes towards pregnancy are always shaded in mystery and indefiniteness.

2) The basic reason for a woman's ambivalent attitude toward pregnancy, writes Simone de Beauvoir in *The Second Sex,* is that "she fears it will mean the loss of her own life."[2] The philosopher Hegel once remarked, "The birth of children is the death of parents." Obstetricians and gynecologists agree that it is normal, even under the very best circumstances, for a woman to have ambivalent and inconsistent feelings about her pregnancy.[3] Dr. H.P. Dunn of New Zealand, on the basis of extensive research, concludes that twice during every pregnancy, a mother will "unwant" her child.

Several significant studies have reported this inconsistent emotional attitude of the pregnant woman. According to Hoerck, 75% of the women who were refused legal abortions in Sweden, in one study, had their babies and were reported to be happy with them.[4] Hook, in a study of 249 Swedish women who were denied legal abortion, reported that 86% gave birth. Of these 249 women, 12% had threatened suicide, but no suicide or even suicide attempts occurred.[5] Kolstad, in a study of 113 women in Norway who were denied legal abortions and carried their pregnancies to term, found that 84% were glad that pregnancy was not terminated.[6]

It is not unusual, report obstetricians, that women experience feelings of resentment, frustration, and depression when they first learn of their pregnant condition. These same women, however, experience positive feelings of acceptance as the pregnancy advances.[7] Most unwanted pregnancies later become wanted babies; some wanted pregnancies become unwanted babies.[8] Rigorous consistency and absolute unambivalence are not associated with a woman's attitude toward her pregnancy or toward her developing unborn child.

3) Pregnancies can be wanted and needed for innumerable wrong reasons. A woman might get pregnant to fortify a liaison

or to strengthen a marriage. She may seek pregnancy to feel whole or to be reassured that she can create. Pregnancy may offer her a spotlight where she can become the center of interest. Helene Deutsch, authoress of some of the most perceptive pages ever written on the psychology of women, writes, "Pregnancy permits woman to rationalize performances which otherwise would appear absurd."[9] A woman might choose pregnancy out of an aching loneliness, out of protest, or out of guilt. A woman may have her reasons, conscious or unconscious, for getting pregnant, but these reasons need not include her child's reason for existing. A child may be wanted or needed to serve only the mother.

* * * * * * * * *

The following question brings each of the above assumptions into common focus: "Can a woman have an ambivalent and inconsistent attitude toward the pregnancy she subconsciously wanted and needed for purely selfish psychological reasons?"

The answer, in effect, has been given in the form of a paper presented to the American College of Obstetricians and Gynecologists by Cornell University of Psychiatrist Lawrence Downs and Psychologist David Clayson.[10]

The authors studied 108 patients who had undergone abortions at New York Hospital. The factor which provided special interest in the study was that most of these women were informed about contraceptives and many had used them. Were these pregnancies both wanted and unwanted?

Compared to 49 women hospitalized for the birth of their first or second babies, all of whom tested normal on the Minnesota Multiphasic Personality Inventory, the aborted women tested as follows: 21% normal; 55% neurotic; 24% psychotic. Furthermore, 85% of the abortion patients had suffered a personal loss, a grave psychiatric distrubance, or both in the months just prior to conception.

These results support the widely held psychiatric belief that pregnancies are rarely unwanted and unneeded. Downs and Clayson concluded that these women unconsciously chose pregnancy as a way of repairing "a threatened or damaged psyche." The pregnancies were needed, but only for a while. Nonetheless, having been wanted or needed had little value for the aborted child.

* * * * * * * * *

Human actions do not submit to being codified by a slogan, especially in matters of sexuality and procreation where men and women act in ways that are both enigmatic and profound. The pithy remark, "Every child should be wanted and needed", is not very illuminating, given the complexity of man and the difficulty of his life. Advice on pregnancy and parental responsibility should be, if it is to be at all helpful, tempered with caution and restraint. It does not honor man's sexual powers to place them on the same irreverent level of sloganeering as political campaigning and commercial advertising.

Slogans are designed to mechanize action by eliminating thinking. Yet, man's most creative act is procreation. To render this act thoughtless and mechanical is to destroy it. An honest and objective assessment of procreation and parenthood can only widen thought and vary action. Sloganized advice on responsible parenthood is both inadequate and misleading. It creates the illusion that human beings operate with machine-like simplicity; it fosters belief in magical cures for what are really formidable problems.

FOOTNOTES

1. Rollo May, *Love and Will* (New York, W.W. Norton & Co., 1969), p. 117.
2. Simone de Beauvoir, *The Second Sex* (New York, Xnopf, 1968), p. 469.
3. Martin Ekblad, "Induced Abortion on Psychiatric Grounds, a Follow-Up Study of 479 Women", *Acta, Psychiat. Neurol. Scand. Suppl.,* 99:238, 1955.
4. Hoerck, cited by Asplund, "Discussion of Swedish Abortion Experience", 11 Buli., *Sloane Hosp.* 77 (1965).
5. K. Hook, "Refused Abortion: A Follow-Up Study of 249 Women Whose Applications Were Refused by the National Board of Health in Sweden", *Acta. Psychiat. Scand.* 39: Suppl. 168, 1963.
6. P. Kolstad, "Therapeutic Abortion: A Clinical Study Based Upon 968 Cases From a Norwegian Hospital, 1950-53", *Acta. Obstet. Gynec. Scand.* 36: Suppl. 6, 1957.
7. Eastman & Hellman, *William's Obstetrics* (New York, Meredith, '66), p. 345.
8. Cf. J. Willke, *Handbook on Abortion* (Cincinnati, Hiltz, '71), p. 48.
9. Helene Deutsch, *The Psychology of Women* (N.Y., Grune & Stratton, 1944), II, 157.
10. *Time,* May 29, 1972.

—34—

SLOGANS, SLOGANEERING AND SLOGANEERS

The word "slogan" is derived from two Scottish words, "sluagh" meaning army and "ghairm", meaning cry. Slogan as "war cry" is well used in the expression, "Sound the fife and cry the slogan, let pibroch fill the air."

The slogan is used most appropriately, as its etymology would indicate, in situations where rational discussion is either irrelevant or impossible. No one discusses things on the battlefield. A slogan is a cry more than an invitation, a signal more than a meaning, an identifying standard more than a universal message. The military character of the slogan is seldom in better evidence than in the sloganeering practiced by pro-abortionists. By an endless barrage of stock slogans, these sloganeers seek not to enlighten their opposition but to weary it into moral insensibility. A modern James Joyce would spell it "slug on". A brief analysis of a representative sample taken from the pro-abortionist stockpile demonstrates the blunt and irrational features of their slogans.

1) "A woman has the right to control her own body." In order to see the hole in this 'argument' all one need do is ask whether it is ethical for a woman to ingest thalidomide during her pregnancy. No man is an island. But is a woman an island?

2) "No one has the right to impose his moral values on another." Yet, when a lady's fine jewelry is stolen, doesn't she immediately impose the seventh commandment on the police force? Aren't anti-abortionists imposed upon when they are compelled to pay higher insurance premiums to help finance other people's abortions?

3) "Unwanted children should not be brought into the world because they might be abused." Dr. Edward Lenoski, Professor of Pediatrics at the University of Southern California, reports that in his 4½ year study of 400 cases of battered children, 90% of the women he surveyed admitted to having planned the preg-

nancies involving the beaten children. Does this mean that all wanted as well as unwanted babies should be aborted in order to prevent child abuse? Dr. Herbert Ratner has termed abortion "child battering in the womb."

4) "No one can decide whether abortion is right or wrong." Does this mean that a Christian humanist who regards all other human beings (including the unborn) as his brothers is not allowed to practice that conviction? Isn't this repression in the most destructive sense of the word? Can anyone decide whether kidnapping is right or wrong? What about foetal kidnapping?

5) "Abortion is a medical matter between a woman and her doctor." Where does this leave fatherhood? The father can merely fertilize but the doctor can exercise the power of veto! After the fact of conception does fatherhood become an irrelevancy? Is pregnancy a privilege or a pathology? Furthermore, the insistence that a physician should be free to perform any operation he chooses within the framework of a physician-patient relationship is an unheard of request for any other profession. Should a lawyer, because his expertise is in law, be granted the private right of changing the law to suit his own and his client's needs?

6) "The foetus is a potential human being whereas the mother is an actual human being." This is a metaphysical distortion. The foetus surely exists. Existence itself is an actuality. Pure potency cannot exist apart from an actualized substance. Pure act exists only in the case of God. Maybe this is why the pro-abortion mother would like to lord over her offspring.

Language is a dangerous instrument. Its misuse in stereotyped slogans, hackneyed cliches, and emotional rhetoric can destroy our authentic relation to things. Preaching the doctrine of the inhumanity and unimportance of the human foetus carries awesome potential dangers to the human race. One immediate danger is to the newly born.

Mary Van Stolk described the personality of the child batterer in her book, *The Battered Child in Canada*. The "dominant cohesive factor" in his personality, she writes, is his "lack of identification with the child as a human being" (Ch. 4). The false premise that denies the humanity of the intrauterine foetus leads to the logical conclusion which permits battering the extra-uterine child. It is unreasonable to expect people to think of the foetus as not human until the doctor cuts the umbilical cord. Only the most superstitious could actually believe that the obstetrician confers humanity. The blurred thinking that makes the doctor God can make the parents behave in a much less than human way.

35

A PROGRESS PROFILE: FROM PREJUDICE TO GENOCIDE THROUGH VIOLENCE

At the Council of the Indies in the early 16th Century, Cardinal Loaysa of Spain decreed, after prolonged deliberation, that the natives of the New World were "no more than parrots" and could be enslaved at will.

A popular expression in America during the Second World War was, "The only good Jap is a dead Jap."

An Indian soldier fighting during the India-Pakistan struggle stated that when he killed an enemy, a beast died; but when one of his men was killed, a human being died.

During the 1969 Columbia University student uprisings, student radicals called policemen "pigs"; the police retaliated by calling the students "monkeys."

Polish people often called the Ukrainians "reptiles". At the same time the Germans referred to their neighbors to the East as "Polish cattle". The Poles responded by calling the Germans "Prussian swine".

There is a saying in Hungary that an Anti-Semite is one who hates Jews more than is absolutely necessary.

German scholars, just prior to the rise of Hitler, defined Jews as sub-humans *(Untermenschen)*, not men at all *(kein Mann)*, and "a phenomenon of putrefaction".

These examples of the combination of prejudice and violence verify its enduring popularity and widespread practice. As history has amply shown, no culture or group of people can consider itself free from prejudice and its threat of violence. And yet, many regard prejudice as an intolerable vice to which they are fortunately immune.

Some young people express indignation at the hypocrisy and prejudice of their elders but, at the same time, admonish one another not to trust anyone over thirty. A student in Massachusetts, no doubt fancying himself to be above prejudice, wrote these words: "The Negro question will never be solved until those dumb white Southerners get something through their ivory skulls."

We usually regard prejudice as a moral vice that infects the other fellow or the other group. Practically no one identifies with Archie Bunker, the comedic bigot in TV's *All in the Family* series. Germain Grisez has stated, "The attitudes of prejudice is not conscious; if it were conscious, it could not be maintained." Nietzsche has remarked, not entirely facetiously, "All prejudices may be tracked back to the intestines." It is not difficult to understand, therefore, why prejudice is so far from eradication. The subject in whom it resides is virtually insensitive to its abiding presence.

Race, color, creed, nationality and sex have long been recognized as barriers which occasion prejudice. But another universal barrier is often overlooked, one that gives rise to the most lethal prejudice ever adopted. This is the birth barrier. Grisez, in the epilogue to his scholarly and compendious work *Abortion: the Myths, the Realities and the Arguments,* writes:

> A new name is needed for prejudice against the unborn; I suggest it be called 'prenatalism' since it is based on the fact we are already born while *they* are unborn (prenatal).

Gordon Allport, in his extensive study *The Nature of Prejudice,* cites five levels of progression through which prejudice develops. They are: *Antilocution* (speaking against someone), *Avoidance, Discrimination, Physical Attack,* and *Extermination.* Prejudice against the human unborn can be brought into sharper focus by applying these five categories to contemporary attitudes toward and actions against him.

1) **Antilocution:** Philosopher Joseph Fletcher states, "There is no such thing as an unborn baby." According to Fletcher the foetus is mere "gametic material". Pro-abortion-evangelist William Baird describes the early foetus as "marmalade". Author Philip Wylie calls the foetus "protoplasmic rubbish", "a gobbet of meat". A political leader announces over the radio that "at twenty weeks' pregnancy you cannot tell the developing fetus from a cancer or a mass of flesh." At a legislative hearing on abortion, university students and faculty members testify that the "foetus is not human. It is a mass of tissue."

Women's Liberation representatives argue that the foetus is part of a woman's body.

On a less physiological level, the human foetus has been termed unwanted, unneeded, an accident, a burden, an inconvenience, an unnecessary expense, a source of distress, a resource depleter, a 'pre-fetus', a 'blueprint', 'garbage', something better off dead than alive.

2) **Avoidance:** In the past few years ecologists and demographers have been issuing bulletins warning the public of the imminent dangers of 'pollution' and 'population explosion'. Along with these alarms has come a concerted emphasis on the urgency of contraceptive birth control. A massive propaganda campaign has advised parents to limit the number of their children in accordance with the ZPG master plan. California biologist Garrett Hardin, in *Science,* attacked the "freedom to breed" and explained the necessity of limiting family size through "mutual coercion, mutually agreed upon by the majority of the people affected." As expectations of a gracious life of affluent mobility soared, stock in children sharply declined. The Age of the Pill had arrived, and the burdens of parenthood could be limited or avoided altogether.

The cynical remark of W.C. Fields that "anyone who hates dogs and children can't be all bad", became more ominous when zero populationist Paul Ehrlich defined the 'mother of the year' as a childless woman who had undergone voluntary hysterectomy. Against a background of antilocution, human offspring began to appear so unattractive a prospect that anti-natalists advocated a reward-punishment system to discourage the "freedom to breed". Bernard Berelson, in a 1969 article, "Beyond Family Planning", proposed the following measures: temporary sterilization administered through the water supply, staple foods, or implanted contraceptive capsules; government licenses to have children; government payments for effectively practicing contraception; tax or welfare penalties for bearing more than a specified number of children.

Mills College valedictorian Stephanie Mills drew wide support and eager disciples after declaring her chosen vocation as an "ex-potential parent". Former Canadian health minister Judy La Marsh told the 1973 YWCA National Convention that perhaps 60 to 70% of women should not bear children. She stated, commenting on the void created by the virtual obsolescence of motherhood:

> It could not be God's will that half the human race should be obsolete, that we should keep a few as breeding factors and that the rest should be unimportant.

3) **Discrimination:** The degeneration of the human foetus having become fashionable and the preventing of his con-

ception having become laudable, the way had been prepared for discrimination. More and more women began to regard their freedom and their "right to choose" as more important than "compulsory pregnancy". The scale of justice tipped in favor of the care, convenience, or career of the mother against the very life of the foetus. Rationalizations gave this kind of thinking social respectability: "The actual life of the mother is more important than the potential life of the foetus;" "every child should be wanted;" "abortion is a private, medical matter between the pregnant woman and her doctor." No longer "nature's finest flower," the foetus became a "parasite" that could be exterminated at will. Pro-abortionists argued that if women were not granted the right to abortion, they themselves would become victims of the government's discrimination. The condition of women's freedom became the right to destroy their unborn.

4) **Physical Attack:** Given the three aforementioned stages of progressive prejudice, it was almost inevitable that laws which forbade abortion were repealed, thereby permitting a wholesale physical attack upon the unborn with curette, suction tube, saline solution, and scalpel.

Statistics Canada reported 542 legal abortions performed in 1969 from August 26 to December 31, the year when the Criminal Code was amended to legalize therapeutic abortions on the recommendation of a hospital committee; 11,152 in 1970; 30,949, in 1971; 38,905 in 1972. One western Canadian hospital had done fewer than 50 abortions between 1966 and 1968, but did 1,207, 2,934, and 3,143 during the years 1970, 1971, and 1972, respectively, while the live births at the same hospital fell during those three years from 3,344 to 2,822 to 2,546.

State officials in California reported 5,000 legal abortions in 1968, the first year of its abortion act; 15,000 the following year; 116,749 in 1971; and an estimated 160,000 in 1972. England's Department of Health reported 27,331 legal abortions in the first year of the Abortion Act, which went into force on April 27, 1968; 36,351 for the slightly longer period from April 27, 1968 to April 30, 1969; 83,850 for 1970; 126,774 for 1971; approximately 150,000 for 1972; and 157,000 for 1973 only six in this year were to save the life of the mother). Before the Abortion Act of 1967, 10,000 abortions a year were being performed.

The New York State figure for legal abortions approached the 200,000 mark in the year and a half following repeal; New York City's figure was 540,245 in its first 30 months following repeal; 208,205 abortions in 1971 (compared to 131,910 live births for the same year). Because of the under-reporting, and the mis-reporting, it is difficult to assess the true number of legal abortions. Newsweek reported an estimated 1,340,000 legal and illegal abortions in the United States in 1971, however, some authorities have estimated that as many as 2,000,000 legal abortions were performed in the United States in 1973.

5) **Extermination:** Some reformers, not satisfied with abortion on request laws, are working for compulsory abortions for entire groups of unborn humans. Kingsley Davis proposed in *Science,* 1967 "a requirement that illegitimate pregnancies be aborted." Black militants and others have interpreted the organization of birth control programs along with other white actions as "a genocidal plot directed against blacks." Patricia Robinson and five of her black sisters reported that "Black women are being asked by militant black brothers not to practice birth control because it is a form of whitey committing genocide on black people." Richard Neuhaus, in his book *In Defense of People,* describes a distinguished medical proponent of abortion who believes that no one should be forced to be born who was not guaranteed "the minimal requirements for a decent existence," namely, "a stable family life, loving parents, quality education, economic security," and so on. The eminent biologist James D. Watson believes that new babies who fail a genetics test should forfeit their right to be born. Pro-abortionist Alan Guttmacher writes, "We are trying to stimulate the creation of wanted children and wanted children only." Lawrence Lader envisions "The right to abortion," establishing "the Century of the Wanted Child."

Thus, the illegitimate, the blacks, the poor, the genetically defective, and the unwanted, like Hitler's "useless eaters", are groups to be exterminated. Human problems are solvable by removing the classes of people who embody the problem. Abortion for genocidal purposes becomes an up-to-date "Final Solution."

* * * * * * * * *

The program to exterminate the unwanted unborn is prejudice in its consummate form of genocidal violence, the logical conclusion to a progression that began with antilocution, defamation, name-calling, slander, and calumny.

It is interesting to note that at the Nuremberg trials, both Rosenberg and Streicher (the philosophers and publicists of the Nazi movement) disclaimed any personal responsibility for the 2½ million Jews who were exterminated at Auschwitz. Colonel Hoess, the officer in charge of the mass murders, however, insisted that it was the incessant propaganda against the Jews which convinced him they deserved extermination. According to Allport:

> It is apparent, therefore, that under certain circumstances there will be a stepwise progression from verbal

aggression to violence, from rumor to riot, from gossip to genocide.

The scientific evidence furnished by genetics, embryology, perinatology, fetology and biology establishes beyond doubt that the growing foetus within the human mother is, from the moment of his conception, an existing, living organism who belongs unequivocally to the species man. To speak of the foetus as sub-human in any way is not only improper and unscientific but also a form of prejudice which marks the beginning of a stepwise progression from antilocution to extermination.

What is most needed in combatting prejudice is a reverence for life that affirms and accepts the natural differences which distinguish one human being from another. To favor any one class on the basis of color, creed, nationality, sex, or birth, is to repudiate the breadth, diversity, and ultimately the total meaning of the human race.

Prejudice is a personal weakness characterized by the ego's reluctance to validate anything noticeably different from itself. In its most extreme form prejudice enacts deicide. When man knows that he rejects his own, he loses faith that God could ever love him. The way to God is through the least of His little ones. Similarly, the way man becomes reconciled to himself is by witnessing, with love and admiration, the humblest of his progeny, the foetus, begin a slow ascent to maturity, revealing through a dramatic step-by-step unfolding sequence, each detail of the glory and wealth which is the human being. The sun at daybreak is no less a sun than hangs in the mid-day sky. The sun at daybreak and the foetus at conception proclaim their being, one syllable at a time.

36

UNIDENTIFIABLE FLYING WORDS

Euphemisms are reality-sweeteners; they make things appear more pleasant thereby making life a little more tolerable and conversation a little less offensive. People feel more comfortable when death is spoken of as "passing away" and the deceased is said to be "laid to rest"; when false teeth are refered to as "dentures" or pimples as "blemishes". It is much easier for a girl to excuse herself if she is going to the "powder-room" than if she is leaving for the toilet.

Euphemisms also create an aura of dignity. An employee feels a sense of elevated status when his position as garbage collector is called "sanitation engineer", or his barber shop a "tonsorial parlor". Some housewives have expressed approval for their title "domestic engineer". Gypsy Rose Lee identified herself for income tax purposes as an "ecdysiast". Bob Newhart jokes about the fellow who holds the ladder for astronauts entering and leaving their spaceship as the man who operates the "ingress-egress transport device".

Another advantage of the euphemism is that it accentuates the positive. Thus, prisoners are "inmates", dull students "slow learners", and retarded children "exceptional". Slums become more respectable as "substandard housing", second hand goods more acceptable as "pre-owned", and artificial pearls more marketable as "cultured pearls".

UFOmisms, on the other hand, are out of this world. Not mere reality-sweeteners, they are reality-distorters; euphemisms carried to the point where, as UFOmisms, there is no longer any resemblance between sign and signified, word and reality. As verbal missiles, they are quite literally Unidentifiable Flying Objects. For example, "adult movie" is often a UFOmism for a pornographic film, as is "healthy sexual experimentation" for promiscuity and "flexible monogomy" for adultery. "A member of the world's oldest profession" is an acceptable euphemism for the prostitute but "therapist", "sexologist", or "masseuse" are irresponsible and misleading UFOmisms.

U.S. military intelligence in Viet Nam produced an official UFOmism of remarkably high unidentifiability — "pacification of the enemy's infrastructure", as a cover-up for blasting the enemy out of their villages. Similarly, the official Nazi expression for consigning six million Jews to death was Final Solution (*endgultige Losung*).

Richard Neuhaus, in his book *In Defense of People,* reports a series of word replacements recommended by a counselor at a New York City abortion clinic: "client" should replace "expectant mother", "problem" should replace 'pregnancy', "termination" should replace 'abortion', and "growth" should replace 'unborn child'. Thus, a counselor is advised to state that, "The doctor has solved the client's problem by terminating the development of an unwanted growth." This bears virtually no semantic resemblance to the more accurate statement of fact, "The doctor has ended the expectant mother's pregnancy by killing her developing unborn child."

T. S. Eliot has stated that, "Human kind cannot bear very much reality". The history of the use of language has born out the truth of this remark. Euphemisms may help make reality more tolerable at times, but their exaggerated use in the form of UFOmisms can make reality difficult to locate. Authentic speaking sometimes requires painful honesty and authentic thinking sometimes requires great courage. Out from the fog built of deceitful verbalizing and timid thinking one may legitimately cry, "What's going on!" Man has a right to know.

Reality disguised by the raiments of unidentifiable verbal smoke screens can be as dangerous as the wolf in sheep's clothing. Poisons should be properly labelled. If education is to lead to enlightenment it must expect more of the student than literacy; it must exact thinking, measuring, comparing, and discovering. It can be very tempting to crawl into a dark cave and cover oneself with a security blanket woven of meaningless words and innocuous phrases. But, though one may turn away from reality, reality will not turn away from him; or, as one philosopher put it, "existence has a way of avenging itself."

VII

A TWIST
OF
IRONY

"Human language is like a cracked kettle on which we beat out tunes for bears to dance to, when all the time we are longing to move the stars to pity."

—Gustave Flaubert

37

THE RADICAL LIBERALS' NOSTRUM FOR AUTOMATICALLY JUSTIFYING JUST ABOUT ANYTHING

"Ignorance", wrote Giordana Bruno, "is one of the most delightful branches of learning. It is acquired without pain and keeps the mind from melancholy." Since it is natural for man to avoid pain and insulate his mind against thoughts which might bring melancholy, it is not surprising that each age has spawned its share of learned ignorance. But today, when learning is so readily available to so many, while the love call of gracious living through technology promises the permanent riddance of pain and melancholy, it would appear that ignorance is enjoying its heyday. All one need do to verify that judgment is take the pains and risk the melancholy to examine the degree of logic which is used by the press, mass media or various impassioned crusaders for so-called liberal causes. Having tried painfully to teach logic over the past five years while suffering no small degree of consequent melancholy, I have observed a growing popularity for a style of arguing which is characterized by a remarkably complete absence of any regard for logic, and an extraordinarily thorough presence of stereotypic rhetoric.

The usual manner of putting forth one's argument today consists in stringing together as many cliches as one can find and enlivening them with "loaded words". To insure the avoidance of thinking, these words are valued either as unconditionally good or unconditionally evil. With this simplistic approach, any 12 year old is prepared to dislodge his parents from time-honored and cherished traditions which required the collective wisdom of the ages to establish. From the list of absolutely good words may be found: freedom, love, conscience, humanitarian, person, right, individual, opportunity, liberate, sympathy, science, minority, etc. When pronounced loudly and confidently these golden words have a magical power to persuade anyone but the most callous misanthrope to the righteousness of the argument. The words of pure evil, which possess the same magical power except they elicit the opposite feelings, include: conform, legislate, Church, medieval, past, impose, judgmental, value-judgment, uptight, obligation, victim, etc.

The following illustrates how an illogical form and a rhetorical content can be brought together with the purpose of conveying credibility. If you can laugh at it, you may never belong to the ranks of the learned ignorant.

The present laws concerning __1__ are obsolete, archaic and impractical. They were established years ago based on social attitudes which are today sorely out-moded. The 'now' generation's views on __2__ are enlightened because they focus on the rights of the __3__ and regard __4__ as a __5__ and not merely a __6__ . A liberal society, freed from the shackles of a medieval mentality, will not be intimidated by the __7__ dogma of __8__ , nor will it kowtow __9__ who are insensitive to __10__ . Furthermore, its citizens will not be made to conform to __11__ values which are __12__ and consequently __13__ .

__14__ have always found a way to __15__ if they so desired in spite of opposing laws. A law which doesn't work and is continually disregarded is no law at all and should be repealed rather than remain to make a mockery of our judicial system. The decision to __16__ is a __17__ one and should involve an individual and his __18__ . The government cannot legislate morality and __19__ is clearly a moral matter. In a civilized society people should be given the freedom to choose for themselves, without governmental interference, concerning matters of morality.

Every __20__ has the right to __21__ but it is a simple fact of life that not every __22__ . When this occurs, it is to show far more compassion for the __23__ by __24__ rather than __25__ only to __26__ . Here __27__ should be allowed by law to follow their consciences and do what must be considered the responsible thing: that is, to __28__ the __29__ .

The public would take a more sympathetic attitude toward the plight of the __30__ once it realized the distress which is caused by __31__ . Furthermore, by making __32__ illegal, we make countless individuals the helpless victims of __33__ . If we are at all humanitarian, and value the quality of life of __34__ , then we should vote to abolish all existing laws which discriminate against __35__ .

175

Content Code

1 abortion
2 abortion
3 mother
4 her
5 person
6 baby machine
7 theological
8 an out-dated church
9 self-righteous moralists
10 any position other than their own
11 Catholic
12 theological
13 unscientific
14 people
15 have an abortion
16 abort
17 medical
18 child is wanted
19 abortion
20 child
21 be born wanted
22 child is wanted
23 foetus
24 having it aborted
25 bring it into an already overcrowded world
26 have it suffer the misery of being rejected
27 women
28 abort
29 unwanted foetus
30 mother
31 bearing an unwanted child
32 abortion
33 underground butchers
34 the mother
35 her

Content

1, 2 suicide
3 individual
4 him
5 man who has the right to control his own body
6 psychopath
7 unbending
8 an irrelevant religion
9 uncompromising moralists
10 the freedom of each person
11 theistic

12 groundless
13 unsupportable
14 people
15 commit suicide
16 take one's life
17 private
18 his conscience
19 suicide
20 person
21 live
22 person wants to go on living
23 individual
24 permitting him to choose death
25 force him to live an unwanted life
26 make him utterly miserable
27 people
28 choose
29 alternative of voluntary death
30 person who no longer finds life valuable
31 being compelled to face a meaningless existence
32 suicide
33 brainwashing shrinks and moralizing clergymen
34 the individual
35 him

Content

1, 2 harmful and addictive drug sales
3 drug addict
4 him
5 human being
6 degenerate
7 out-moded
8 an uptight state
9 narrow minded squares
10 the pleasures of drugs
11 middle class
12 hypocritical
13 meaningless
14 drug users
15 get drugs
16 become a chronic drug user
17 personal
18 his private value-system
19 drug use
20 person
21 live a sober and drug free life
22 wants this
23 drug addict
24 allowing him to take drugs

25 force him to live according to the life styles of others
26 make him frustrated and depressed
27 drug addicts
28 make
29 scene
30 addict
31 making his next fix so difficult, so uncertain, and so unsafe
32 the sale of harmful and addictive drugs
33 unscrupulous drug pushers and unfair drug laws
34 the drug addict
35 him

Content

1 prostitution
2 prostitution
3 career woman
4 her
5 sensuous woman
6 body used for the convenient gratification of men
7 sexist
8 a puritanistic society
9 the sexually effete
10 the pleasures of sexuality
11 Victorian
12 fearful of the human body
13 degrade love making
14 prostitutes
15 meet their clients
16 choose prostitution as a career
17 socio-economic
18 her vocational director
19 prostitution
20 woman
21 reject prostitution as a career
22 woman is willing to be employed in some other capacity
23 woman
24 allowing her to become a professional sex consultant
25 forbid her to earn money from her act
26 render her sexual relationships unprofitable
27 women
28 select
29 career of their choice
30 prostitute
31 trying to earn a decent living within an over-restrictive legal system
32 prostitution
33 unsanitary working conditions and a vicious name-calling public

34 the prostitute
35 her

Content

1, 2 organized crime
3 criminal
4 him
5 person
6 plague upon society
7 rigid
8 parochial politics
9 one-sided rulers
10 the way other people may look at life
11 capitalistic
12 monopolistic
13 undemocratic
14 criminals
15 spread crime
16 join an underground crime syndicate
17 family
18 "Godfather"
19 organized crime
20 community
21 be adequately safeguarded against crime
22 community has within its budget sufficient funds for such a measure
23 community
24 allowing organized crime to operate
25 to allocate tremendous sums of money for law enforcement
26 cripple the community economically
27 criminals
28 maintain
29 only expression of justice and professionalism that they know
30 criminal
31 putting in an honest day's work and earning a low salary most of which is either withheld by the government or eaten up by inflation
32 organized crime
33 police brutality and prisons which degrade rather than rehabilitate
34 organized criminals
35 them

Content

1 shop-lifting
2 shop-lifting
3 shop-lifter

4 him
5 consumer
6 common thief
7 heartless
8 the business world
9 its smug representatives
10 the needs of the poor
11 corporational
12 bureaucratic
13 inhuman
14 the needy
15 shop-lift
16 shop-lift
17 financial
18 his needs
19 shop-lifting
20 store owner
21 be protected against shop-lifting
22 storeowner can afford to pay the price required for such protection
23 storeowner
24 allowing shop-lifting to take place
25 require him to pay exorbitant protection costs
26 have him lose more money in the end
27 shop-lifters
28 take
29 goods they need
30 indigent shop-lifter
31 being poor
32 shop-lifting
33 unfeeling security guards and snooping store detectives
34 the shop-lifter
35 him

Content

1 cannibalism
2 cannibalism
3 cannibal
4 him
5 discriminating epicure
6 barbaric carnivore
7 hollow
8 the past
9 stodgy vegetarians
10 the pure delights of cannibalism to say nothing of its dietary advantages
11 religious
12 arbitrary
13 questionable

14 cannibals
15 practice their art
16 practice cannibalism
17 cultural
18 his tribal mores
19 cannibalism
20 person
21 to be protected against cannibalism
22 person can be, especially in remote and inaccessible places
23 victim
24 allowing him to be fed to cannibals
25 keep him alive momentarily
26 have him die eventually, probably of some disease in such a
    way as to benefit no one
27 cannibals
28 enjoy
29 gourmet art for which they are so well known
30 cannibal
31 the exorbitant price of meat these days
32 cannibalism
33 an assortment of dietary deficiency ailments
34 the cannibal
35 him

38

UPDATING THE HIPPOCRATIC OATH

In recent months, a number of medical men throughout North America have openly expressed their disenchantment with the *Hippocratic Oath*. Particularly distressing to them is the occurrence of the phrase "I will not give to a woman an instrument to practice abortion." Quite clearly, this bit of archaic idealism does not square with what's actually going on in so many North American hospitals and abortion clinics. Furthermore, this oath, if rigidly upheld, would deprive many medically trained personnel of a healthy source of income. In addition, the retention of the *Hippocratic Oath* as it stands, could lead to the re-emergence of the 'guilty conscience syndrome', a malady which modern psychology has proven to be purely the creation of authoritarian religious institutions. Therefore, with the best concern for all, I would like to make the following suggestion. Rather than make doctors feel trapped by the moral rhetoric of an outdated oath, we should give them the freedom to select whichever oath best suits their personal, medical, and financial needs. At the same time, since doctors have a strong nostalgia for the glorious history of the medical profession, the updated oaths should bear some resemblance, in name at least, to the *Hippocratic Oath*. I propose the following six oaths as appropriately modernized replacements for the one supplied by a well intentioned but rather shortsighted ancient Greek Physician.

1) **The Hypocritical Oath:** Although I am trained to heal, care for, protect and safeguard human life through the knowledge and skills of my medical art, I may, whenever it suits my purpose, practice that art in a way which contradicts all the aims of my training.

2) **The Hypothetical Oath:** If it is convenient for me to heal through the practice of my medical art, I shall. If it isn't I won't.

3) **The Hippopancratic Oath:** ('Hippo' and 'pan' are derived from the Greek words for 'horse' and 'around'). I will usually practice my medical art in a way consonant with the ideals expressed in the *Hippocratic Oath,* but I will leave some opportunity for 'horsing around'.

4) **The Hippiecratic Oath:** I do solemnly swear to uphold my right as long as I practice the sacred art of medicine, to "do my own thing."

5) **The Hippodromic Oath:** My training in the holy law and art of medicine has been long, arduous and costly. In my career as a doctor I will do my utmost to reverse the pattern by seeing to it that in treating patients things are always quick, easy, and lucrative.

6) **The Hypercritical Oath:** I faithfully promise to remain excessively critical of any oath which commits me to a positive attitude toward life or living human beings in the practice of my medical art.

39

THE SOCIETY FOR A HUMAN CONTINUANCE

It is very exciting to be living at a moment in history when man is standing at the very threshold of his full humanity. The love children, the children of peace, are showing us the way to human liberation. We are finally realizing that violence, war, greed, and wealth fail to satisfy man's inner needs.

The liberal movements both political and social are winning the war for the full human on the battlefield of love and reason. In particular, the women's liberation movement is helping to assert the right of every woman to achieve the full measure of her humanity. It is high time that every woman be given the freedom to control her own body. Only then can she become a truly self-determining human being. It is high time that every child who is brought into the world is met with love and warmth. Only then does a child have an honest chance of becoming a full human being.

As an extension of the wave of human liberation, I have founded the Society for a Human Continuance. Our credo is: "Every infant has a right to continue to grow as a human being; every parent has a right to continue a happy marriage."

To be perfectly realistic, not every married couple makes good parents. Many sincere, well-meaning people marry, have a baby, and suddenly realize that they just weren't cut out for rearing children. We at SHC feel that an unwanted child is an unhappy child and burdened parents are bothered parents.

It is therefore the goal of the Society for a Human Continuance to effect the repeal of the current outmoded laws which forbid infanticide. The decision to carry out a "discretionary quietus" should be made by the parents and an authorized and duly qualified social counselor. The government has no right to interfere in personal matters between parent and infant.

When legislation respects the freedom of parents to make private moral decisions, our society will have taken a giant stride toward the liberation of full human beings. It is far more moral to release an unhappy and unwelcome infant from this world than to compel him to remain in a family situation that can only add to his misery and that of everyone around him.

We do not view the legalization of infanticide as a rejection of the value of human life. Removing a restriction from law is not the same as removing a person from life. Rather, we view infanticide as primarily a moral matter, not a legal one, which must be made by the individuals most directly involved.

What a happier world it would be if parents were not hamstrung by legal restrictions and children were not condemned to a life of rejection.

B. Elsie Bubb

Founder and Director,
Society for a Human Continuance

—40—

"A NIGHT TO REMEMBER": A MODERNIZED FABLE

Abigail Feenly is living peacefully today in a small New Hampshire town. Recently she celebrated her 70th birthday with her five children, their spouses, and all twenty-four of her two dozen beautiful grandchildren. Abigail is a kind of celebrity in her family. She was one of the 705 survivors of the *Titanic* disaster. The most curious piece of memorabilia she has preserved from that cold night in 1912 is a parched and faded sheet of paper on which her father hastily had pencilled an urgent statement. However, fate intervened just moments before that statement was to be presented to the captain and converted an urgent message into a puzzling keepsake.

Osgood Feenly was, in the opinion of his friends, charming in manner, fastidious in appearance, and liberal in thought. A perfectionist, he would often go to painstaking extremes to ensure making the desired impression. He took great pride in his highly responsible position as executive vice-president of a distinguished New York City brokerage firm. It was no doubt this professionally cultivated sense of responsibility that led him to assume competence in deciding the order of placing passengers on the few available life-boats.

According to his daughter Abigail's recollection, Osgood, in true character, was memorizing and rehearsing his "Who Shall Be Saved" statement in front of the bathroom mirror when he was swept to his untimely death by a flood of water that had burst through the ceiling immediately over his head. Abigail, standing close to the doorway, was knocked safely into the hallway. When she was able to return to the room to search for her father, she found but his scribbled legacy — the timeless document.

"Who Shall Be Saved"

"You are the captain; the commander-in-chief of this ship. But it is most urgent that you listen to me so that one tragedy does not lead to a greater one. I overheard you give the order to save the women and children first. An admirable gesture! But this is not an occasion for a display of medieval gallantry; nor is it a time to be carried away by form and sentimentality. Hard as it may be, you must stand firm by the side of unbiased reason.

The first class section of this sinking ship includes a rare and extraordinary assemblage of men. Their importance to the people on the mainland and the people of the future is inestimable. It is within your power to grant these men a privilege they have so richly deserved — to continue serving mankind as they have done so generously in the past.

I dearly love my family and I myself am not afraid to die, but this is a time for realistic decision-making. We live in a world governed by men and it is the men of social prominence in particular whose service to mankind is far greater and longer lasting than the service, as important as it may be, that is contributed by women, children, and men of little or no status.

Allow those who have already succeeded in life to safeguard that success rather than save but those whose present is relatively unformed and whose future is only a vague potentiality.

I entreat you, Captain, to allow the men in first class to enter the life-boats first. Their talents are most important; their survival is most needed."

It is a matter of record that the majority of the survivors were women and children. Osgood Feenly never presented his statement and a different, more traditional set of criteria was applied. The irony of that April tragedy in 1912 was that the ship was not titanic but many of its passengers indeed were.

41

A BRIEF REPORT CONCERNING LIFE ON THE "BLUE PLANET"

The committee representing the *Bureau of Inter-galactic Space Travel* has completed its study of life on the "Blue Planet". The study was undertaken in behalf of the *World-to World Inter-galactic Space Program* (WISP) to determine the ethical implications of destroying the existing life there and converting the planet into a re-fueling station and observation center. The committee has concluded that life on the "Blue Planet" should be terminated since its continuance would represent a serious inconvenience to projected plans in space travel.

A brief description of the "Blue Planet's" most advanced form of life is set forth below establishing beyond any dispute that its primitive structure and lowly nature do not give it the right to intrude upon space projects of the magnitude and significance of WISP. The committee has named this form of life Phaethon, since it is sired by the sun (Helios) and is destined for extinction by a super-terrestrial power (Zeus struck down Phaethon with thunder bolts).

1) Phaethon has never communicated with intelligent life on another planet. It is a pre-socialized being. Indeed, it is not even aware that other intelligent life exists in the universe.

2) Phaethon is strictly dependent on its immediate environment for its life supporting substances. Oxygen, food and water, indispensable for its survival, must be continuously assimilated from the circumambient air, the circumjacent terrain, and the circumferential seas. A few brief trips by small teams of specialists to a nearby satellite notwithstanding, Phaethon must be regarded as virtually a planetary parasite.

3) Phaethon may be said to have potential for life outside its solar system but as yet has conceived no actual way of freeing itself from its natural restrictions of time, space, and gravitation. It can not be considered viable outside its solar system.

4) In height, weight, and size, Phaethon is an undistinguished trifle. Its movements are slow and sluggish, its intelligence meager, its life-span brief. It can be described as a short-lived, struggling blob of usually unconscious protoplasm. Phaethon's eradication will be neither missed nor mourned.

5) Regarding physical integrity, Phaethon has not discovered a way of preventing gross deformities and serious diseases from weakening its species. Through the ages, the cumulative effect of permitting deformed and diseased members to survive has been an unfortunate pollution of the gene pool. Phaethon's sudden and painless extinction would spare it the ignominy of a steady and complete genetic deterioration.

Some morally scrupulous individuals may argue that removing humble Phaethon from the universe would be an unethical act, violently terminating, no matter how miserable, the only form of life which the powers of the universe had granted that creature. The committee feels that sensible and realistic individuals will evaluate Paethon's demise not as a loss but as a gain for WISP and all who will profit from the "Blue Planet's" participation in inter-galactic affairs. Moreover, Phaethon will be re-channeled into a higher good which represents, in the last analysis, a greater and more enduring value than that which Phaethon could experience in the few remaining years it had before the forces of nature would have inevitably intervened.

42

LIBERATION

Take from me my baby, and give me opportunity;
My love's too large to have it lost on life that's in its infancy;
I've made appointments for my love with cultured aristocracy.

Take from me my pregnancy and grant me infertility;
My life's too broad to be defined by the corners of a nursery;
I've reservations for my life with the corners of the galaxy.

Take from me my burden and give my life simplicity;
My youth's too eager to have it drained in suffering and
        uncertainty;
I've planned my youth to feel the bliss of joy without
        complexity.

Remove that blight, that curse, that cross which limits my
        prosperity;
I'll take the open attitude that reaches for infinity;
And damn that Power Who's said to be made perfect in my
        infirmity.

ACKNOWLEDGMENTS

Writing a book is usually a corporate venture. Unless the author writes on a deserted island, in solitary confinement, or under some highly unusual set of restricting circumstances, he invariably enlists the help of anyone around him who possesses even the meagerest interest in his subject matter. The writing of this book has been a corporate venture, but it has also been a personally gratifying community experience; and I wish to thank my circle of co-contributers, co-advisors, and co-pilots, whose interest in the abortion issue is indeed sizeable, for both their capable academic assistance and their esteemed personal friendship.

Most of the essays in this work have been previously published in more or less altered versions in a variety of journals, magazines, and papers. I thank the editors of the following publications for the encouragement they gave me, and their valuable criticisms and suggestions: *Linacre Quarterly, American Ecclesiastical Review, Review for Religious, Sisters Today, Our Family, Marriage, Triumph, Messenger of the Sacred Heart, The Cambrdige Fish, The Canadian Register, The Catholic Register, Our Sunday Visitor, The Mennonite Reporter, The Wanderer, Catholic Currents, The Canadian Layman, The Uncertified Human, Ancaster News, The Kitchener-Waterloo Record, The Stratford Times, Serviam, The Life Guardian, Griffin House,* and others.

I also thank, for time and again supplying me with invaluable research materials, Madeline and Yvon Gaboury, Mary Nowak, Joseph Monahan, Judith Vanderkooy, and Dr. Hart and Marilyn Bezner. For their assistance in so many different yet equally important ways I thank Dr. Edoardo Evans, Angelo Gualtieri, Dr. Gerard Campbell, Rev. John Ford, Drs. Ruth and Igor Levitsky, Dr. Ho, Sister Leon, Dr. F.F. Centore, Dr. Heather Morris, Rev. Dr. Paul Marx, John E. Harrington, Drs. Martin Estall, Herbert Ratner, and L. L. deVeber, and most especially my ever-near companion and least flattering critic, my wife Mary.

I thank Dr. and Mrs. Willke, and Rev. Dr. Donald McCarthy for their patient work in reading and processing my manuscript; secretaries Susan Wickware, Connie Pierce, Shawn Ashley, and Elaine Voisin for their clerical assistance; librarians Marguerite and Mary Beth Reinhardt for a variety of services; and Bob Vezina, Larry Henderson, Denyse Handler, and Rev. Peter Fehrenbach, C. R. for their personal and public support.

My most humble thanks to artist William Kurelek for his illustrations and cultural philosopher Marshall McLuhan for writing the Foreword.

I thank, quite sincerely, the many who have strenuously opposed my views on abortion. Quite often I was forced to develop deeper insights as a result of encountering their strong resistance. While they may be less willing to receive my thanks than I am to extend them, I acknowledge their indirect contribution nonetheless.

Last, and most of all, with more thanks than I know how to offer, I thank Virginia D. Gager, the best English stylist I have ever had the pleasure of knowing. Her interest in my work and her most generous reading and correcting of my manuscript literally transformed an unpublishable work into a publishable one.

Donald DeMarco
Kitchener, Ontario
July 7, 1974

OTHER PUBLICATIONS
by
Hiltz & Hayes Publishing Co.

On Sexuality:

SEX, Should We Wait —

A live recording of a dialogue with 500 young people on the subject of sex before marriage.

Cassettes & Manual 11.50

The WONDER of SEX

A love and family centered book to help parents teach their children.

Paperback .... .95

The Wonder of Sex Records

A recording of an evening on sex education of children.

L.P. Records 6.95

SEX EDUCATION — The How-To For Teachers

For teachers, parents, and professionals, a guide book on how sexuality is really taught, how to (and how not to) set up a school program and how to teach controversial subjects.

Paperback 2.50

On Abortion

ABORTION, HOW IT IS

A strikingly convincing presentation of medical, social, and historical facts defending the right to life of the unborn.

2 Cassettes, 24 Slides 19.95
1 Cass., Manual, 24 Slides . 14.95

LIFE OR DEATH

A full color brochure showing live developing babies and dead aborted ones. Factual, full documentation, for volume distribution.

1000 Brochures 75.00

DID YOU KNOW

A small, full color brochure, a mini *Life or Death,* fits in envelope.

1000 Copies 20.00

The U.S. Supreme Court Said

Color brochure explaining the decision on abortion and calling for action.

1000 Copies 75.00

How To Teach the Pro Life Story

Teaching techniques, words, methods, materials, exhibiting, TV and radio, etc.

Paperback 2.95

All of the above by Dr. & Mrs. J.C. Willke